THIS IS YOUR **PASSBOOK**® FOR ...

LEGAL SECRETARIAL ASSISTANT

NATIONAL LEARNING CORPORATION®
passbooks.com

PASSBOOK® SERIES

THE *PASSBOOK® SERIES* has been created to prepare applicants and candidates for the ultimate academic battlefield – the examination room.

At some time in our lives, each and every one of us may be required to take an examination – for validation, matriculation, admission, qualification, registration, certification, or licensure.

Based on the assumption that every applicant or candidate has met the basic formal educational standards, has taken the required number of courses, and read the necessary texts, the *PASSBOOK® SERIES* furnishes the one special preparation which may assure passing with confidence, instead of failing with insecurity. Examination questions – together with answers – are furnished as the basic vehicle for study so that the mysteries of the examination and its compounding difficulties may be eliminated or diminished by a sure method.

This book is meant to help you pass your examination provided that you qualify and are serious in your objective.

The entire field is reviewed through the huge store of content information which is succinctly presented through a provocative and challenging approach – the question-and-answer method.

A climate of success is established by furnishing the correct answers at the end of each test.

You soon learn to recognize types of questions, forms of questions, and patterns of questioning. You may even begin to anticipate expected outcomes.

You perceive that many questions are repeated or adapted so that you can gain acute insights, which may enable you to score many sure points.

You learn how to confront new questions, or types of questions, and to attack them confidently and work out the correct answers.

You note objectives and emphases, and recognize pitfalls and dangers, so that you may make positive educational adjustments.

Moreover, you are kept fully informed in relation to new concepts, methods, practices, and directions in the field.

You discover that you arre actually taking the examination all the time: you are preparing for the examination by "taking" an examination, not by reading extraneous and/or supererogatory textbooks.

In short, this PASSBOOK®, used directedly, should be an important factor in helping you to pass your test.

LEGAL SECRETARIAL ASSISTANT

JOB DESCRIPTION

This class of positions encompasses responsible secretarial, typing and related office activities utilizing manual and automated office systems in a legal environment.

Under supervision, with some latitude for independent judgment, performs moderately difficult secretarial and typing duties, types briefs, memoranda, legal documents and statistical reports; operates modern word processing equipment used in the processing of legal documents and correspondence; proofreads legal briefs, reports, documents, and other correspondence; answers phones, places calls and transmits information for attorneys; maintains legal files and other pertinent legal documents; may transcribe from tapes; may take dictation and transcribe notes; may serve as a secretary as assigned; may assist in training staff.

SCOPE OF THE EXAMINATION

The written test will be of the multiple-choice type and may include questions on reading comprehension; filing and record keeping; English language usage; general office procedures; and related areas.

The typing test will consist of typing from typed copy at a minimum speed of 55 words per minute for five minutes. In order to achieve a passing score, candidates are allowed no more than eight (8) errors (spelling, punctuation, etc.) for each 275 typed words.

HOW TO TAKE A TEST

I. YOU MUST PASS AN EXAMINATION

A. *WHAT EVERY CANDIDATE SHOULD KNOW*

Examination applicants often ask us for help in preparing for the written test. What can I study in advance? What kinds of questions will be asked? How will the test be given? How will the papers be graded?

As an applicant for a civil service examination, you may be wondering about some of these things. Our purpose here is to suggest effective methods of advance study and to describe civil service examinations.

Your chances for success on this examination can be increased if you know how to prepare. Those "pre-examination jitters" can be reduced if you know what to expect. You can even experience an adventure in good citizenship if you know why civil service exams are given.

B. *WHY ARE CIVIL SERVICE EXAMINATIONS GIVEN?*

Civil service examinations are important to you in two ways. As a citizen, you want public jobs filled by employees who know how to do their work. As a job seeker, you want a fair chance to compete for that job on an equal footing with other candidates. The best-known means of accomplishing this two-fold goal is the competitive examination.

Exams are widely publicized throughout the nation. They may be administered for jobs in federal, state, city, municipal, town or village governments or agencies.

Any citizen may apply, with some limitations, such as the age or residence of applicants. Your experience and education may be reviewed to see whether you meet the requirements for the particular examination. When these requirements exist, they are reasonable and applied consistently to all applicants. Thus, a competitive examination may cause you some uneasiness now, but it is your privilege and safeguard.

C. *HOW ARE CIVIL SERVICE EXAMS DEVELOPED?*

Examinations are carefully written by trained technicians who are specialists in the field known as "psychological measurement," in consultation with recognized authorities in the field of work that the test will cover. These experts recommend the subject matter areas or skills to be tested; only those knowledges or skills important to your success on the job are included. The most reliable books and source materials available are used as references. Together, the experts and technicians judge the difficulty level of the questions.

Test technicians know how to phrase questions so that the problem is clearly stated. Their ethics do not permit "trick" or "catch" questions. Questions may have been tried out on sample groups, or subjected to statistical analysis, to determine their usefulness.

Written tests are often used in combination with performance tests, ratings of training and experience, and oral interviews. All of these measures combine to form the best-known means of finding the right person for the right job.

II. HOW TO PASS THE WRITTEN TEST

A. NATURE OF THE EXAMINATION

To prepare intelligently for civil service examinations, you should know how they differ from school examinations you have taken. In school you were assigned certain definite pages to read or subjects to cover. The examination questions were quite detailed and usually emphasized memory. Civil service exams, on the other hand, try to discover your present ability to perform the duties of a position, plus your potentiality to learn these duties. In other words, a civil service exam attempts to predict how successful you will be. Questions cover such a broad area that they cannot be as minute and detailed as school exam questions.

In the public service similar kinds of work, or positions, are grouped together in one "class." This process is known as *position-classification*. All the positions in a class are paid according to the salary range for that class. One class title covers all of these positions, and they are all tested by the same examination.

B. FOUR BASIC STEPS

1) Study the announcement

How, then, can you know what subjects to study? Our best answer is: "Learn as much as possible about the class of positions for which you've applied." The exam will test the knowledge, skills and abilities needed to do the work.

Your most valuable source of information about the position you want is the official exam announcement. This announcement lists the training and experience qualifications. Check these standards and apply only if you come reasonably close to meeting them.

The brief description of the position in the examination announcement offers some clues to the subjects which will be tested. Think about the job itself. Review the duties in your mind. Can you perform them, or are there some in which you are rusty? Fill in the blank spots in your preparation.

Many jurisdictions preview the written test in the exam announcement by including a section called "Knowledge and Abilities Required," "Scope of the Examination," or some similar heading. Here you will find out specifically what fields will be tested.

2) Review your own background

Once you learn in general what the position is all about, and what you need to know to do the work, ask yourself which subjects you already know fairly well and which need improvement. You may wonder whether to concentrate on improving your strong areas or on building some background in your fields of weakness. When the announcement has specified "some knowledge" or "considerable knowledge," or has used adjectives like "beginning principles of..." or "advanced ... methods," you can get a clue as to the number and difficulty of questions to be asked in any given field. More questions, and hence broader coverage, would be included for those subjects which are more important in the work. Now weigh your strengths and weaknesses against the job requirements and prepare accordingly.

3) Determine the level of the position

Another way to tell how intensively you should prepare is to understand the level of the job for which you are applying. Is it the entering level? In other words, is this the position in which beginners in a field of work are hired? Or is it an intermediate or advanced level? Sometimes this is indicated by such words as "Junior" or "Senior" in the class title. Other jurisdictions use Roman numerals to designate the level – Clerk I, Clerk II, for example. The word "Supervisor" sometimes appears in the title. If the level is not indicated by the title, check the description of duties. Will you be working under very close supervision, or will you have responsibility for independent decisions in this work?

4) Choose appropriate study materials

Now that you know the subjects to be examined and the relative amount of each subject to be covered, you can choose suitable study materials. For beginning level jobs, or even advanced ones, if you have a pronounced weakness in some aspect of your training, read a modern, standard textbook in that field. Be sure it is up to date and has general coverage. Such books are normally available at your library, and the librarian will be glad to help you locate one. For entry-level positions, questions of appropriate difficulty are chosen – neither highly advanced questions, nor those too simple. Such questions require careful thought but not advanced training.

If the position for which you are applying is technical or advanced, you will read more advanced, specialized material. If you are already familiar with the basic principles of your field, elementary textbooks would waste your time. Concentrate on advanced textbooks and technical periodicals. Think through the concepts and review difficult problems in your field.

These are all general sources. You can get more ideas on your own initiative, following these leads. For example, training manuals and publications of the government agency which employs workers in your field can be useful, particularly for technical and professional positions. A letter or visit to the government department involved may result in more specific study suggestions, and certainly will provide you with a more definite idea of the exact nature of the position you are seeking.

III. KINDS OF TESTS

Tests are used for purposes other than measuring knowledge and ability to perform specified duties. For some positions, it is equally important to test ability to make adjustments to new situations or to profit from training. In others, basic mental abilities not dependent on information are essential. Questions which test these things may not appear as pertinent to the duties of the position as those which test for knowledge and information. Yet they are often highly important parts of a fair examination. For very general questions, it is almost impossible to help you direct your study efforts. What we can do is to point out some of the more common of these general abilities needed in public service positions and describe some typical questions.

1) General information

Broad, general information has been found useful for predicting job success in some kinds of work. This is tested in a variety of ways, from vocabulary lists to questions about current events. Basic background in some field of work, such as sociology or economics, may be sampled in a group of questions. Often these are principles which have become familiar to most persons through exposure rather than through formal training. It is difficult to advise you how to study for these questions; being alert to the world around you is our best suggestion.

2) Verbal ability

An example of an ability needed in many positions is verbal or language ability. Verbal ability is, in brief, the ability to use and understand words. Vocabulary and grammar tests are typical measures of this ability. Reading comprehension or paragraph interpretation questions are common in many kinds of civil service tests. You are given a paragraph of written material and asked to find its central meaning.

3) Numerical ability

Number skills can be tested by the familiar arithmetic problem, by checking paired lists of numbers to see which are alike and which are different, or by interpreting charts and graphs. In the latter test, a graph may be printed in the test booklet which you are asked to use as the basis for answering questions.

4) Observation

A popular test for law-enforcement positions is the observation test. A picture is shown to you for several minutes, then taken away. Questions about the picture test your ability to observe both details and larger elements.

5) Following directions

In many positions in the public service, the employee must be able to carry out written instructions dependably and accurately. You may be given a chart with several columns, each column listing a variety of information. The questions require you to carry out directions involving the information given in the chart.

6) Skills and aptitudes

Performance tests effectively measure some manual skills and aptitudes. When the skill is one in which you are trained, such as typing or shorthand, you can practice. These tests are often very much like those given in business school or high school courses. For many of the other skills and aptitudes, however, no short-time preparation can be made. Skills and abilities natural to you or that you have developed throughout your lifetime are being tested.

Many of the general questions just described provide all the data needed to answer the questions and ask you to use your reasoning ability to find the answers. Your best preparation for these tests, as well as for tests of facts and ideas, is to be at your physical and mental best. You, no doubt, have your own methods of getting into an exam-taking mood and keeping "in shape." The next section lists some ideas on this subject.

IV. KINDS OF QUESTIONS

Only rarely is the "essay" question, which you answer in narrative form, used in civil service tests. Civil service tests are usually of the short-answer type. Full instructions for answering these questions will be given to you at the examination. But in case this is your first experience with short-answer questions and separate answer sheets, here is what you need to know:

1) Multiple-choice Questions

Most popular of the short-answer questions is the "multiple choice" or "best answer" question. It can be used, for example, to test for factual knowledge, ability to solve problems or judgment in meeting situations found at work.

A multiple-choice question is normally one of three types—

- It can begin with an incomplete statement followed by several possible endings. You are to find the one ending which *best* completes the statement, although some of the others may not be entirely wrong.
- It can also be a complete statement in the form of a question which is answered by choosing one of the statements listed.
- It can be in the form of a problem – again you select the best answer.

Here is an example of a multiple-choice question with a discussion which should give you some clues as to the method for choosing the right answer:

When an employee has a complaint about his assignment, the action which will *best* help him overcome his difficulty is to
A. discuss his difficulty with his coworkers
B. take the problem to the head of the organization
C. take the problem to the person who gave him the assignment
D. say nothing to anyone about his complaint

In answering this question, you should study each of the choices to find which is best. Consider choice "A" – Certainly an employee may discuss his complaint with fellow employees, but no change or improvement can result, and the complaint remains unresolved. Choice "B" is a poor choice since the head of the organization probably does not know what assignment you have been given, and taking your problem to him is known as "going over the head" of the supervisor. The supervisor, or person who made the assignment, is the person who can clarify it or correct any injustice. Choice "C" is, therefore, correct. To say nothing, as in choice "D," is unwise. Supervisors have and interest in knowing the problems employees are facing, and the employee is seeking a solution to his problem.

2) True/False Questions

The "true/false" or "right/wrong" form of question is sometimes used. Here a complete statement is given. Your job is to decide whether the statement is right or wrong.

SAMPLE: A roaming cell-phone call to a nearby city costs less than a non-roaming call to a distant city.

This statement is wrong, or false, since roaming calls are more expensive.
This is not a complete list of all possible question forms, although most of the others are variations of these common types. You will always get complete directions for

answering questions. Be sure you understand *how* to mark your answers – ask questions until you do.

V. RECORDING YOUR ANSWERS

Computer terminals are used more and more today for many different kinds of exams.

For an examination with very few applicants, you may be told to record your answers in the test booklet itself. Separate answer sheets are much more common. If this separate answer sheet is to be scored by machine – and this is often the case – it is highly important that you mark your answers correctly in order to get credit.

An electronic scoring machine is often used in civil service offices because of the speed with which papers can be scored. Machine-scored answer sheets must be marked with a pencil, which will be given to you. This pencil has a high graphite content which responds to the electronic scoring machine. As a matter of fact, stray dots may register as answers, so do not let your pencil rest on the answer sheet while you are pondering the correct answer. Also, if your pencil lead breaks or is otherwise defective, ask for another.

Since the answer sheet will be dropped in a slot in the scoring machine, be careful not to bend the corners or get the paper crumpled.

The answer sheet normally has five vertical columns of numbers, with 30 numbers to a column. These numbers correspond to the question numbers in your test booklet. After each number, going across the page are four or five pairs of dotted lines. These short dotted lines have small letters or numbers above them. The first two pairs may also have a "T" or "F" above the letters. This indicates that the first two pairs only are to be used if the questions are of the true-false type. If the questions are multiple choice, disregard the "T" and "F" and pay attention only to the small letters or numbers.

Answer your questions in the manner of the sample that follows:

32. The largest city in the United States is
    A. Washington, D.C.
    B. New York City
    C. Chicago
    D. Detroit
    E. San Francisco

1) Choose the answer you think is best. (New York City is the largest, so "B" is correct.)
2) Find the row of dotted lines numbered the same as the question you are answering. (Find row number 32)
3) Find the pair of dotted lines corresponding to the answer. (Find the pair of lines under the mark "B.")
4) Make a solid black mark between the dotted lines.

VI. BEFORE THE TEST

Common sense will help you find procedures to follow to get ready for an examination. Too many of us, however, overlook these sensible measures. Indeed, nervousness and fatigue have been found to be the most serious reasons why applicants fail to do their best on civil service tests. Here is a list of reminders:

- Begin your preparation early – Don't wait until the last minute to go scurrying around for books and materials or to find out what the position is all about.
- Prepare continuously – An hour a night for a week is better than an all-night cram session. This has been definitely established. What is more, a night a week for a month will return better dividends than crowding your study into a shorter period of time.
- Locate the place of the exam – You have been sent a notice telling you when and where to report for the examination. If the location is in a different town or otherwise unfamiliar to you, it would be well to inquire the best route and learn something about the building.
- Relax the night before the test – Allow your mind to rest. Do not study at all that night. Plan some mild recreation or diversion; then go to bed early and get a good night's sleep.
- Get up early enough to make a leisurely trip to the place for the test – This way unforeseen events, traffic snarls, unfamiliar buildings, etc. will not upset you.
- Dress comfortably – A written test is not a fashion show. You will be known by number and not by name, so wear something comfortable.
- Leave excess paraphernalia at home – Shopping bags and odd bundles will get in your way. You need bring only the items mentioned in the official notice you received; usually everything you need is provided. Do not bring reference books to the exam. They will only confuse those last minutes and be taken away from you when in the test room.
- Arrive somewhat ahead of time – If because of transportation schedules you must get there very early, bring a newspaper or magazine to take your mind off yourself while waiting.
- Locate the examination room – When you have found the proper room, you will be directed to the seat or part of the room where you will sit. Sometimes you are given a sheet of instructions to read while you are waiting. Do not fill out any forms until you are told to do so; just read them and be prepared.
- Relax and prepare to listen to the instructions
- If you have any physical problem that may keep you from doing your best, be sure to tell the test administrator. If you are sick or in poor health, you really cannot do your best on the exam. You can come back and take the test some other time.

VII. AT THE TEST

The day of the test is here and you have the test booklet in your hand. The temptation to get going is very strong. Caution! There is more to success than knowing the right answers. You must know how to identify your papers and understand variations in the type of short-answer question used in this particular examination. Follow these suggestions for maximum results from your efforts:

1) Cooperate with the monitor

The test administrator has a duty to create a situation in which you can be as much at ease as possible. He will give instructions, tell you when to begin, check to see that you are marking your answer sheet correctly, and so on. He is not there to guard you, although he will see that your competitors do not take unfair advantage. He wants to help you do your best.

2) Listen to all instructions

Don't jump the gun! Wait until you understand all directions. In most civil service tests you get more time than you need to answer the questions. So don't be in a hurry. Read each word of instructions until you clearly understand the meaning. Study the examples, listen to all announcements and follow directions. Ask questions if you do not understand what to do.

3) Identify your papers

Civil service exams are usually identified by number only. You will be assigned a number; you must not put your name on your test papers. Be sure to copy your number correctly. Since more than one exam may be given, copy your exact examination title.

4) Plan your time

Unless you are told that a test is a "speed" or "rate of work" test, speed itself is usually not important. Time enough to answer all the questions will be provided, but this does not mean that you have all day. An overall time limit has been set. Divide the total time (in minutes) by the number of questions to determine the approximate time you have for each question.

5) Do not linger over difficult questions

If you come across a difficult question, mark it with a paper clip (useful to have along) and come back to it when you have been through the booklet. One caution if you do this – be sure to skip a number on your answer sheet as well. Check often to be sure that you have not lost your place and that you are marking in the row numbered the same as the question you are answering.

6) Read the questions

Be sure you know what the question asks! Many capable people are unsuccessful because they failed to *read* the questions correctly.

7) Answer all questions

Unless you have been instructed that a penalty will be deducted for incorrect answers, it is better to guess than to omit a question.

8) Speed tests

It is often better NOT to guess on speed tests. It has been found that on timed tests people are tempted to spend the last few seconds before time is called in marking answers at random – without even reading them – in the hope of picking up a few extra points. To discourage this practice, the instructions may warn you that your score will be "corrected" for guessing. That is, a penalty will be applied. The incorrect answers will be deducted from the correct ones, or some other penalty formula will be used.

9) Review your answers

If you finish before time is called, go back to the questions you guessed or omitted to give them further thought. Review other answers if you have time.

10) Return your test materials

If you are ready to leave before others have finished or time is called, take ALL your materials to the monitor and leave quietly. Never take any test material with you. The monitor can discover whose papers are not complete, and taking a test booklet may be grounds for disqualification.

VIII. EXAMINATION TECHNIQUES

1) Read the general instructions carefully. These are usually printed on the first page of the exam booklet. As a rule, these instructions refer to the timing of the examination; the fact that you should not start work until the signal and must stop work at a signal, etc. If there are any *special* instructions, such as a choice of questions to be answered, make sure that you note this instruction carefully.

2) When you are ready to start work on the examination, that is as soon as the signal has been given, read the instructions to each question booklet, underline any key words or phrases, such as *least*, *best*, *outline*, *describe* and the like. In this way you will tend to answer as requested rather than discover on reviewing your paper that you *listed without describing*, that you selected the *worst* choice rather than the *best* choice, etc.

3) If the examination is of the objective or multiple-choice type – that is, each question will also give a series of possible answers: A, B, C or D, and you are called upon to select the best answer and write the letter next to that answer on your answer paper – it is advisable to start answering each question in turn. There may be anywhere from 50 to 100 such questions in the three or four hours allotted and you can see how much time would be taken if you read through all the questions before beginning to answer any. Furthermore, if you come across a question or group of questions which you know would be difficult to answer, it would undoubtedly affect your handling of all the other questions.

4) If the examination is of the essay type and contains but a few questions, it is a moot point as to whether you should read all the questions before starting to answer any one. Of course, if you are given a choice – say five out of seven and the like – then it is essential to read all the questions so you can eliminate the two that are most difficult. If, however, you are asked to answer all the questions, there may be danger in trying to answer the easiest one first because you may find that you will spend too much time on it. The best technique is to answer the first question, then proceed to the second, etc.

5) Time your answers. Before the exam begins, write down the time it started, then add the time allowed for the examination and write down the time it must be completed, then divide the time available somewhat as follows:

- If 3-1/2 hours are allowed, that would be 210 minutes. If you have 80 objective-type questions, that would be an average of 2-1/2 minutes per question. Allow yourself no more than 2 minutes per question, or a total of 160 minutes, which will permit about 50 minutes to review.
- If for the time allotment of 210 minutes there are 7 essay questions to answer, that would average about 30 minutes a question. Give yourself only 25 minutes per question so that you have about 35 minutes to review.

6) The most important instruction is to *read each question* and make sure you know what is wanted. The second most important instruction is to *time yourself properly* so that you answer every question. The third most important instruction is to *answer every question*. Guess if you have to but include something for each question. Remember that you will receive no credit for a blank and will probably receive some credit if you write something in answer to an essay question. If you guess a letter – say "B" for a multiple-choice question – you may have guessed right. If you leave a blank as an answer to a multiple-choice question, the examiners may respect your feelings but it will not add a point to your score. Some exams may penalize you for wrong answers, so in such cases *only*, you may not want to guess unless you have some basis for your answer.

7) Suggestions
   a. Objective-type questions
      1. Examine the question booklet for proper sequence of pages and questions
      2. Read all instructions carefully
      3. Skip any question which seems too difficult; return to it after all other questions have been answered
      4. Apportion your time properly; do not spend too much time on any single question or group of questions
      5. Note and underline key words – *all, most, fewest, least, best, worst, same, opposite*, etc.
      6. Pay particular attention to negatives
      7. Note unusual option, e.g., unduly long, short, complex, different or similar in content to the body of the question
      8. Observe the use of "hedging" words – *probably, may, most likely*, etc.
      9. Make sure that your answer is put next to the same number as the question
      10. Do not second-guess unless you have good reason to believe the second answer is definitely more correct
      11. Cross out original answer if you decide another answer is more accurate; do not erase until you are ready to hand your paper in
      12. Answer all questions; guess unless instructed otherwise
      13. Leave time for review

   b. Essay questions
      1. Read each question carefully
      2. Determine exactly what is wanted. Underline key words or phrases.
      3. Decide on outline or paragraph answer

4. Include many different points and elements unless asked to develop any one or two points or elements
5. Show impartiality by giving pros and cons unless directed to select one side only
6. Make and write down any assumptions you find necessary to answer the questions
7. Watch your English, grammar, punctuation and choice of words
8. Time your answers; don't crowd material

8) Answering the essay question

Most essay questions can be answered by framing the specific response around several key words or ideas. Here are a few such key words or ideas:

M's: manpower, materials, methods, money, management
P's: purpose, program, policy, plan, procedure, practice, problems, pitfalls, personnel, public relations

   a. Six basic steps in handling problems:
     1. Preliminary plan and background development
     2. Collect information, data and facts
     3. Analyze and interpret information, data and facts
     4. Analyze and develop solutions as well as make recommendations
     5. Prepare report and sell recommendations
     6. Install recommendations and follow up effectiveness

   b. Pitfalls to avoid
     1. *Taking things for granted* – A statement of the situation does not necessarily imply that each of the elements is necessarily true; for example, a complaint may be invalid and biased so that all that can be taken for granted is that a complaint has been registered
     2. *Considering only one side of a situation* – Wherever possible, indicate several alternatives and then point out the reasons you selected the best one
     3. *Failing to indicate follow up* – Whenever your answer indicates action on your part, make certain that you will take proper follow-up action to see how successful your recommendations, procedures or actions turn out to be
     4. *Taking too long in answering any single question* – Remember to time your answers properly

IX. AFTER THE TEST

Scoring procedures differ in detail among civil service jurisdictions although the general principles are the same. Whether the papers are hand-scored or graded by machine we have described, they are nearly always graded by number. That is, the person who marks the paper knows only the number – never the name – of the applicant. Not until all the papers have been graded will they be matched with names. If other tests, such as training and experience or oral interview ratings have been given, scores will be combined. Different parts of the examination usually have different weights. For example, the written test might count 60 percent of the final grade, and a rating of training and experience 40 percent. In many jurisdictions, veterans will have a certain number of points added to their grades.

After the final grade has been determined, the names are placed in grade order and an eligible list is established. There are various methods for resolving ties between those who get the same final grade – probably the most common is to place first the name of the person whose application was received first. Job offers are made from the eligible list in the order the names appear on it. You will be notified of your grade and your rank as soon as all these computations have been made. This will be done as rapidly as possible.

People who are found to meet the requirements in the announcement are called "eligibles." Their names are put on a list of eligible candidates. An eligible's chances of getting a job depend on how high he stands on this list and how fast agencies are filling jobs from the list.

When a job is to be filled from a list of eligibles, the agency asks for the names of people on the list of eligibles for that job. When the civil service commission receives this request, it sends to the agency the names of the three people highest on this list. Or, if the job to be filled has specialized requirements, the office sends the agency the names of the top three persons who meet these requirements from the general list.

The appointing officer makes a choice from among the three people whose names were sent to him. If the selected person accepts the appointment, the names of the others are put back on the list to be considered for future openings.

That is the rule in hiring from all kinds of eligible lists, whether they are for typist, carpenter, chemist, or something else. For every vacancy, the appointing officer has his choice of any one of the top three eligibles on the list. This explains why the person whose name is on top of the list sometimes does not get an appointment when some of the persons lower on the list do. If the appointing officer chooses the second or third eligible, the No. 1 eligible does not get a job at once, but stays on the list until he is appointed or the list is terminated.

X. HOW TO PASS THE INTERVIEW TEST

The examination for which you applied requires an oral interview test. You have already taken the written test and you are now being called for the interview test – the final part of the formal examination.

You may think that it is not possible to prepare for an interview test and that there are no procedures to follow during an interview. Our purpose is to point out some things you can do in advance that will help you and some good rules to follow and pitfalls to avoid while you are being interviewed.

What is an interview supposed to test?

The written examination is designed to test the technical knowledge and competence of the candidate; the oral is designed to evaluate intangible qualities, not readily measured otherwise, and to establish a list showing the relative fitness of each candidate – as measured against his competitors – for the position sought. Scoring is not on the basis of "right" and "wrong," but on a sliding scale of values ranging from "not passable" to "outstanding." As a matter of fact, it is possible to achieve a relatively low score without a single "incorrect" answer because of evident weakness in the qualities being measured.

Occasionally, an examination may consist entirely of an oral test – either an individual or a group oral. In such cases, information is sought concerning the technical knowledges and abilities of the candidate, since there has been no written examination for this purpose. More commonly, however, an oral test is used to supplement a written examination.

Who conducts interviews?

The composition of oral boards varies among different jurisdictions. In nearly all, a representative of the personnel department serves as chairman. One of the members of the board may be a representative of the department in which the candidate would work. In some cases, "outside experts" are used, and, frequently, a businessman or some other representative of the general public is asked to serve. Labor and management or other special groups may be represented. The aim is to secure the services of experts in the appropriate field.

However the board is composed, it is a good idea (and not at all improper or unethical) to ascertain in advance of the interview who the members are and what groups they represent. When you are introduced to them, you will have some idea of their backgrounds and interests, and at least you will not stutter and stammer over their names.

What should be done before the interview?

While knowledge about the board members is useful and takes some of the surprise element out of the interview, there is other preparation which is more substantive. It *is* possible to prepare for an oral interview – in several ways:

1) Keep a copy of your application and review it carefully before the interview

This may be the only document before the oral board, and the starting point of the interview. Know what education and experience you have listed there, and the sequence and dates of all of it. Sometimes the board will ask you to review the highlights of your experience for them; you should not have to hem and haw doing it.

2) Study the class specification and the examination announcement

Usually, the oral board has one or both of these to guide them. The qualities, characteristics or knowledges required by the position sought are stated in these documents. They offer valuable clues as to the nature of the oral interview. For example, if the job involves supervisory responsibilities, the announcement will usually indicate that knowledge of modern supervisory methods and the qualifications of the candidate as a supervisor will be tested. If so, you can expect such questions, frequently in the form of a hypothetical situation which you are expected to solve. NEVER go into an oral without knowledge of the duties and responsibilities of the job you seek.

3) Think through each qualification required

Try to visualize the kind of questions you would ask if you were a board member. How well could you answer them? Try especially to appraise your own knowledge and background in each area, *measured against the job sought*, and identify any areas in which you are weak. Be critical and realistic – do not flatter yourself.

4) Do some general reading in areas in which you feel you may be weak

For example, if the job involves supervision and your past experience has NOT, some general reading in supervisory methods and practices, particularly in the field of human relations, might be useful. Do NOT study agency procedures or detailed manuals. The oral board will be testing your understanding and capacity, not your memory.

5) Get a good night's sleep and watch your general health and mental attitude

You will want a clear head at the interview. Take care of a cold or any other minor ailment, and of course, no hangovers.

What should be done on the day of the interview?

Now comes the day of the interview itself. Give yourself plenty of time to get there. Plan to arrive somewhat ahead of the scheduled time, particularly if your appointment is in the fore part of the day. If a previous candidate fails to appear, the board might be ready for you a bit early. By early afternoon an oral board is almost invariably behind schedule if there are many candidates, and you may have to wait. Take along a book or magazine to read, or your application to review, but leave any extraneous material in the waiting room when you go in for your interview. In any event, relax and compose yourself.

The matter of dress is important. The board is forming impressions about you – from your experience, your manners, your attitude, and your appearance. Give your personal appearance careful attention. Dress your best, but not your flashiest. Choose conservative, appropriate clothing, and be sure it is immaculate. This is a business interview, and your appearance should indicate that you regard it as such. Besides, being well groomed and properly dressed will help boost your confidence.

Sooner or later, someone will call your name and escort you into the interview room. *This is it.* From here on you are on your own. It is too late for any more preparation. But remember, you asked for this opportunity to prove your fitness, and you are here because your request was granted.

What happens when you go in?

The usual sequence of events will be as follows: The clerk (who is often the board stenographer) will introduce you to the chairman of the oral board, who will introduce you to the other members of the board. Acknowledge the introductions before you sit down. Do not be surprised if you find a microphone facing you or a stenotypist sitting by. Oral interviews are usually recorded in the event of an appeal or other review.

Usually the chairman of the board will open the interview by reviewing the highlights of your education and work experience from your application – primarily for the benefit of the other members of the board, as well as to get the material into the record. Do not interrupt or comment unless there is an error or significant misinterpretation; if that is the case, do not hesitate. But do not quibble about insignificant matters. Also, he will usually ask you some question about your education, experience or your present job – partly to get you to start talking and to establish the interviewing "rapport." He may start the actual questioning, or turn it over to one of the other members. Frequently, each member undertakes the questioning on a particular area, one in which he is perhaps most competent, so you can expect each member to participate in the examination. Because time is limited, you may also expect some rather abrupt switches in the direction the questioning takes, so do not be upset by it. Normally, a board member will not pursue a single line of questioning unless he discovers a particular strength or weakness.

After each member has participated, the chairman will usually ask whether any member has any further questions, then will ask you if you have anything you wish to add. Unless you are expecting this question, it may floor you. Worse, it may start you off on an extended, extemporaneous speech. The board is not usually seeking more information. The question is principally to offer you a last opportunity to present further qualifications or to indicate that you have nothing to add. So, if you feel that a significant qualification or characteristic has been overlooked, it is proper to point it out in a sentence or so. Do not compliment the board on the thoroughness of their examination – they have been sketchy, and you know it. If you wish, merely say, "No thank you, I have nothing further to add." This is a point where you can "talk yourself out" of a good impression or fail to present an important bit of information. Remember, *you close the interview yourself.*

The chairman will then say, "That is all, Mr. _____, thank you." Do not be startled; the interview is over, and quicker than you think. Thank him, gather your belongings and take your leave. Save your sigh of relief for the other side of the door.

How to put your best foot forward

Throughout this entire process, you may feel that the board individually and collectively is trying to pierce your defenses, seek out your hidden weaknesses and embarrass and confuse you. Actually, this is not true. They are obliged to make an appraisal of your qualifications for the job you are seeking, and they want to see you in your best light. Remember, they must interview all candidates and a non-cooperative candidate may become a failure in spite of their best efforts to bring out his qualifications. Here are 15 suggestions that will help you:

1) Be natural – Keep your attitude confident, not cocky

If you are not confident that you can do the job, do not expect the board to be. Do not apologize for your weaknesses, try to bring out your strong points. The board is interested in a positive, not negative, presentation. Cockiness will antagonize any board member and make him wonder if you are covering up a weakness by a false show of strength.

2) Get comfortable, but don't lounge or sprawl

Sit erectly but not stiffly. A careless posture may lead the board to conclude that you are careless in other things, or at least that you are not impressed by the importance of the occasion. Either conclusion is natural, even if incorrect. Do not fuss with your clothing, a pencil or an ashtray. Your hands may occasionally be useful to emphasize a point; do not let them become a point of distraction.

3) Do not wisecrack or make small talk

This is a serious situation, and your attitude should show that you consider it as such. Further, the time of the board is limited – they do not want to waste it, and neither should you.

4) Do not exaggerate your experience or abilities

In the first place, from information in the application or other interviews and sources, the board may know more about you than you think. Secondly, you probably will not get away with it. An experienced board is rather adept at spotting such a situation, so do not take the chance.

5) If you know a board member, do not make a point of it, yet do not hide it

Certainly you are not fooling him, and probably not the other members of the board. Do not try to take advantage of your acquaintanceship – it will probably do you little good.

6) Do not dominate the interview

Let the board do that. They will give you the clues – do not assume that you have to do all the talking. Realize that the board has a number of questions to ask you, and do not try to take up all the interview time by showing off your extensive knowledge of the answer to the first one.

7) Be attentive

You only have 20 minutes or so, and you should keep your attention at its sharpest throughout. When a member is addressing a problem or question to you, give him your undivided attention. Address your reply principally to him, but do not exclude the other board members.

8) Do not interrupt

A board member may be stating a problem for you to analyze. He will ask you a question when the time comes. Let him state the problem, and wait for the question.

9) Make sure you understand the question

Do not try to answer until you are sure what the question is. If it is not clear, restate it in your own words or ask the board member to clarify it for you. However, do not haggle about minor elements.

10) Reply promptly but not hastily

A common entry on oral board rating sheets is "candidate responded readily," or "candidate hesitated in replies." Respond as promptly and quickly as you can, but do not jump to a hasty, ill-considered answer.

11) Do not be peremptory in your answers

A brief answer is proper – but do not fire your answer back. That is a losing game from your point of view. The board member can probably ask questions much faster than you can answer them.

12) Do not try to create the answer you think the board member wants

He is interested in what kind of mind you have and how it works – not in playing games. Furthermore, he can usually spot this practice and will actually grade you down on it.

13) Do not switch sides in your reply merely to agree with a board member

Frequently, a member will take a contrary position merely to draw you out and to see if you are willing and able to defend your point of view. Do not start a debate, yet do not surrender a good position. If a position is worth taking, it is worth defending.

14) Do not be afraid to admit an error in judgment if you are shown to be wrong

The board knows that you are forced to reply without any opportunity for careful consideration. Your answer may be demonstrably wrong. If so, admit it and get on with the interview.

15) Do not dwell at length on your present job

The opening question may relate to your present assignment. Answer the question but do not go into an extended discussion. You are being examined for a *new* job, not your present one. As a matter of fact, try to phrase ALL your answers in terms of the job for which you are being examined.

Basis of Rating

Probably you will forget most of these "do's" and "don'ts" when you walk into the oral interview room. Even remembering them all will not ensure you a passing grade. Perhaps you did not have the qualifications in the first place. But remembering them will help you to put your best foot forward, without treading on the toes of the board members.

Rumor and popular opinion to the contrary notwithstanding, an oral board wants you to make the best appearance possible. They know you are under pressure – but they also want to see how you respond to it as a guide to what your reaction would be under the pressures of the job you seek. They will be influenced by the degree of poise you display, the personal traits you show and the manner in which you respond.

ABOUT THIS BOOK

This book contains tests divided into Examination Sections. Go through each test, answering every question in the margin. At the end of each test look at the answer key and check your answers. On the ones you got wrong, look at the right answer choice and learn. Do not fill in the answers first. Do not memorize the questions and answers, but understand the answer and principles involved. On your test, the questions will likely be different from the samples. Questions are changed and new ones added. If you understand these past questions you should have success with any changes that arise. Tests may consist of several types of questions. We have additional books on each subject should more study be advisable or necessary for you. Finally, the more you study, the better prepared you will be. This book is intended to be the last thing you study before you walk into the examination room. Prior study of relevant texts is also recommended. NLC publishes some of these in our Fundamental Series. Knowledge and good sense are important factors in passing your exam. Good luck also helps. So now study this Passbook, absorb the material contained within and take that knowledge into the examination. Then do your best to pass that exam.

EXAMINATION SECTION

EXAMINATION SECTION
TEST 1

DIRECTIONS: Each question or incomplete statement is followed by several suggested answers or completions. Select the one that BEST answers the question or completes the statement. *PRINT THE LETTER OF THE CORRECT ANSWER IN THE SPACE AT THE RIGHT.*

Questions 1-9.

DIRECTIONS: Questions 1 through 9 consist of sentences which may or may not be examples of good English usage. Consider grammar, punctuation, spelling, capitalization, awkwardness, etc. Examine each sentence, and then choose the correct statement about it from the four choices below it. If the English usage in the sentence given is better than it would be with any of the changes suggested in options B, C, and D, choose option A. Do not choose an option that will change the meaning of the sentence.

1. According to Judge Frank, the grocer's sons found guilty of assault and sentenced last Thursday.
    A. This is an example of acceptable writing.
    B. A comma should be placed after the word *sentenced.*
    C. The word *were* should be placed after *sons*
    D. The apostrophe in *grocer's* should be placed after the *s.*

1.____

2. The department heads assistant said that the stenographers should type duplicate copies of all contracts, leases, and bills.
    A. This is an example of acceptable writing.
    B. A comma should be placed before the word *contracts.*
    C. An apostrophe should be placed before the *s* in *heads.*
    D. Quotation marks should be placed before *the stenographers* and after *bills.*

2.____

3. The lawyers questioned the men to determine who was the true property owner?
    A. This is an example of acceptable writing.
    B. The phrase *questioned the men* should be changed to *asked the men questions.*
    C. The word *was* should be changed to *were.*
    D. The question mark should be changed to a period.

3.____

4. The terms stated in the present contract are more specific than those stated in the previous contract.
    A. This is an example of acceptable writing.
    B. The word *are* should be changed to *is.*
    C. The word *than* should be changed to *then.*
    D. The word *specific* should be changed to *specified.*

4.____

5. Of the lawyers considered, the one who argued more skillful was chosen for the job.
    A. This is an example of acceptable writing.
    B. The word *more* should be replaced by the word *most.*
    C. The word *skillful* should be replaced by the word *skillfully,*
    D. The word *chosen* should be replaced by the word *selected.*

5.____

1

6. Each of the states has a court of appeals; some states have circuit courts.   6.____

    A. This is an example of acceptable writing.
    B. The semi-colon should be changed to a comma.
    C. The word *has* should be changed to *have*.
    D. The word *some* should be capitalized.

7. The court trial has greatly effected the child's mental condition.   7.____

    A. This is an example of acceptable writing.
    B. The word *effected* should be changed to *affected*.
    C. The word *greatly* should be placed after *effected*.
    D. The apostrophe in *child's* should be placed after the *s*.

8. Last week, the petition signed by all the officers was sent to the Better Business Bureau.   8.____

    A. This is an example of acceptable writing.
    B. The phrase *last week* should be placed after *officers*.
    C. A comma should be placed after *petition*.
    D. The word *was* should be changed to *were*.

9. Mr. Farrell claims that he requested form A-12, and three booklets describing court pro-   9.____
cedures.

    A. This is an example of acceptable writing.
    B. The word *that* should be eliminated.
    C. A colon should be placed after *requested*.
    D. The comma after *A-12* should be eliminated.

Questions 10-21.

DIRECTIONS: Questions 10 through 21 contain a word in capital letters followed by four suggested meanings of the word. For each question, choose the BEST meaning
for the word in capital letters.

10. SIGNATORY - A   10.____

    A. lawyer who draws up a legal document
    B. document that must be signed by a judge
    C. person who signs a document
    D. true copy of a signature

11. RETAINER - A   11.____

    A. fee paid to a lawyer for his services
    B. document held by a third party
    C. court decision to send a prisoner back to custody pending trial
    D. legal requirement to keep certain types of files

12. BEQUEATH - To   12.____

    A. receive assistance from a charitable organization
    B. give personal property by will to another
    C. transfer real property from one person to another
    D. receive an inheritance upon the death of a relative

13. RATIFY - To   13._____

    A. approve and sanction   B. forego
    C. produce evidence   D. summarize

14. CODICIL - A   14._____

    A. document introduced in evidence in a civil action
    B. subsection of a law
    C. type of legal action that can be brought by a plaintiff
    D. supplement or an addition to a will

15. ALIAS   15._____

    A. Assumed name   B. In favor of
    C. Against   D. A writ

16. PROXY - A(n)   16._____

    A. phony document in a real estate transaction
    B. opinion by a judge of a civil court
    C. document containing appointment of an agent
    D. summons in a lawsuit

17. ALLEGED   17._____

    A. Innocent   B. Asserted
    C. Guilty   D. Called upon

18. EXECUTE - To   18._____

    A. complete a legal document by signing it
    B. set requirements
    C. render services to a duly elected executive of a municipality
    D. initiate legal action such as a lawsuit

19. NOTARY PUBLIC - A   19._____

    A. lawyer who is running for public office
    B. judge who hears minor cases
    C. public officer, one of whose functions is to administer oaths
    D. lawyer who gives free legal services to persons unable to pay

20. WAIVE - To   20._____

    A. disturb a calm state of affairs
    B. knowingly renounce a right or claim
    C. pardon someone for a minor fault
    D. purposely mislead a person during an investigation

21. ARRAIGN - To   21._____

    A. prevent an escape   B. defend a prisoner
    C. verify a document   D. accuse in a court of law

Questions 22-40.

DIRECTIONS: Questions 22 through 40 each consist of four words which may or may not be
spelled correctly. If you find an error in
only one word, mark your answer A;
any two words, mark your answer B;
any three words, mark your answer C;
none of these words, mark your answer D.

22.	occurrence	Febuary	privilege	similiar	22.____
23.	separate	transferring	analyze	column	23.____
24.	develop	license	bankrupcy	abreviate	24.____
25.	subpoena	arguement	dissolution	foreclosure	25.____
26.	exaggerate	fundamental	significance	warrant	26.____
27.	citizen	endorsed	marraige	appraissal	27.____
28.	precedant	univercity	observence	preliminary	28.____
29.	stipulate	negligence	judgment	prominent	29.____
30.	judisial	whereas	release	guardian	30.____
31.	appeal	larcenny	transcrip	jurist	31.____
32.	petition	tenancy	agenda	insurance	32.____
33.	superfical	premise	morgaged	maintainance	33.____
34.	testamony	publically	installment	possessed	34.____
35.	escrow	decree	eviction	miscelaneous	35.____
36.	securitys	abeyance	adhere	corporate	36.____
37.	kaleidoscope	anesthesia	vermilion	tafetta	37.____
38.	congruant	barrenness	plebescite	vigilance	38.____
39.	picnicing	promisory	resevoir	omission	39.____
40.	supersede	banister	wholly	seize	40.____

KEY (CORRECT ANSWERS)

1.	C	11.	A	21.	D	31.	B
2.	C	12.	B	22.	B	32.	D
3.	D	13.	A	23.	D	33.	C
4.	A	14.	D	24.	B	34.	B
5.	C	15.	A	25.	A	35.	A
6.	A	16.	C	26.	D	36.	A
7.	B	17.	B	27.	B	37.	A
8.	A	18.	A	28.	C	38.	B
9.	D	19.	C	29.	D	39.	C
10.	C	20.	B	30.	A	40.	D

EXAMINATION SECTION
TEST 1

DIRECTIONS: Each question or incomplete statement is followed by several suggested answers or completions. Select the one that BEST answers the question or completes the statement. *PRINT THE LETTER OF THE CORRECT ANSWER IN THE SPACE AT THE RIGHT.*

Questions 1-6.

DIRECTIONS: Questions 1 through 6 consist of descriptions of material to which a filing designation must be assigned.

Assume that the matters and cases described in the questions were referred for handling to a government legal office which has its files set up according to these file designations. The file designation consists of a number of characters and punctuation marks as described below.

The first character refers to agencies whose legal work is handled by this office. These agencies are numbered consecutively in the order in which they first submit a matter for attention, and are identified in an alphabetical card index. To date numbers have been assigned to agencies as follows:

Department of Correction	1
Police Department	2
Department of Traffic	3
Department of Consumer Affairs	4
Commission on Human Rights	5
Board of Elections	6
Department of Personnel	7
Board of Estimate	8

The second character is separated from the first character by a dash. The second character is the last digit of the year in which a particular lawsuit or matter is referred to the legal office.

The third character is separated from the second character by a colon and may consist of either of the following:

I. *A sub-number assigned to each lawsuit to which the agency is a party. Lawsuits are numbered consecutively regardless of year. (Lawsuits are brought by or against agency heads rather than agencies themselves, but references are made to agencies for the purpose of simplification.)*

or II. *A capital letter assigned to each matter other than a lawsuit according to subject, the subject being identified in an alphabetical index. To date, letters have been assigned to subjects as follows:*

Citizenship	A	Housing	E
Discrimination	B	Gambling	F
Residence Requirements	C	Freedom of Religion	G
Civil Service Examinations	D		

These referrals are numbered consecutively regardless of year. The first referral by a particular agency on citizenship, for example, would be designated A1, followed by A2, A3, etc.

If no reference is made in a question as to how many letters involving a certain subject or how many lawsuits have been referred by an agency, assume that it is the first.

For each question, choose the file designation which is MOST appropriate for filing the material described in the question.

1. In January 2010, two candidates in a 2009 civil service examination for positions with the Department of Correction filed a suit against the Department of Personnel seeking to set aside an educational requirement for the title.
    The Department of Personnel immediately referred the lawsuit to the legal office for handling.

    A. 1-9:1   B. 1-0:D1   C. 7-9:D1   D. 7-0:1   1._____

2. In 2014, the Police Department made its sixth request for an opinion on whether an employee assignment proposed for 2015 could be considered discriminatory.

    A. 2-5:1-B6   B. 2-4:6   C. 2-4:1-B6   D. 2-4:B6   2._____

3. In 2015, a lawsuit was brought by the Bay Island Action Committee against the Board of Estimate in which the plaintiff sought withdrawal of approval of housing for the elderly in the Bay Island area given by the Board in 2015.

    A. 8-3:1   B. 8-5:1   C. 8-3:B1   D. 8-5:E1   3._____

4. In December 2014, community leaders asked the Police Department to ban outdoor meetings of a religious group on the grounds that the meetings were disrupting the area. Such meetings had been held from time to time during 2014. On January 31, 2015, the Police Department asked the government legal office for an opinion on whether granting this request would violate the worshippers' right to freedom of religion.

    A. 2-4:G-1   B. 2-5:G1   C. 2-5:B-1   D. 2-4:B1   4._____

5. In 2014, a woman filed suit against the Board of Elections. She alleged that she had not been permitted to vote at her usual polling place in the 2013 election and had been told she was not registered there. She claimed that she had always voted there and that her record card had been lost. This was the fourth case of its type for this agency.

    A. 6-4:4   B. 6-3:C4   C. 3-4:6   D. 6-3:4   5._____

6. A lawsuit was brought in 2011 by the Ace Pinball Machine Company against the Commissioner of Consumer Affairs. The lawsuit contested an ordinance which banned the use of pinball machines on the ground that they are gambling devices.
    This was the third lawsuit to which the Department of Consumer Affairs was a party.

    A. 4-1:1   B. 4-3:F1   C. 4-1:3   D. 3F-4:1   6._____

8

7. You are instructed by your supervisor to type a statement that must be signed by the person making the statement and by three witnesses to the signature. The typed statement will take two pages and will leave no room for signatures if the normal margin is maintained at the bottom of the second page.
In this situation, the PREFERRED method is to type

    A. the signature lines below the normal margin on the second page
    B. nothing further and have the witnesses sign without a typed signature line
    C. the signature lines on a third page
    D. some of the text and the signature lines on a third page

7.____

8. Certain legal documents always begin with a statement of venue - that is, the county and state in which the document is executed. This is usually boxed with a parentheses or colons.
The one of the following documents that ALWAYS bears a statement of venue in a prominent position at its head is a(n)

    A. affidavit   B. memorandum of law
    C. contract of sale   D. will

8.____

9. A court stenographer is to take stenographic notes and transcribe the statements of a person under oath. The person has a heavy accent and speaks in ungrammatical and broken English.
When he or she is transcribing the testimony, of the following, the BEST thing for them to do is to

    A. transcribe the testimony exactly as spoken, making no grammatical changes
    B. make only the grammatical changes which would clarify the client's statements
    C. make all grammatical changes so that the testimony is in standard English form
    D. ask the client's permission before making any grammatical changes

9.____

10. When the material typed on a printed form does not fill the space provided, a Z-ruling is frequently drawn to fill up the unused space.
The MAIN purpose of this practice is to

    A. make the document more pleasing to the eye
    B. indicate that the preceding material is correct
    C. insure that the document is not altered
    D. show that the lawyer has read it

10.____

11. After you had typed an original and five copies of a certain document, some changes were made in ink on the original and were initialed by all the parties. The original was signed by all the parties, and the signatures were notarized.
Which of the following should *generally* be typed on the copies BEFORE filing the original and the copies? The inked changes

    A. but not the signatures, initials, or notarial data
    B. the signatures and the initials but not the notarial data
    C. and the notarial data but not the signatures or initials
    D. the signatures, the initials, and the notarial data

11.____

12. The first paragraph of a noncourt agreement *generally* contains all of the following EXCEPT the   12.____

    A. specific terms of the agreement
    B. date of the agreement
    C. purpose of the agreement
    D. names of the parties involved

13. When typing an answer in a court proceeding, the place where the word ANSWER should be typed on the first page of the document is   13.____

    A. at the upper left-hand corner
    B. below the index number and to the right of the box containing the names of the parties to the action
    C. above the index number and to the right of the box containing the names of the parties to the action
    D. to the left of the names of the attorneys for the defendant

14. Which one of the following statements BEST describes the legal document called an acknowledgment?   14.____
It is

    A. an answer to an affidavit
    B. a receipt issued by the court when a document is filed
    C. proof of service of a summons
    D. a declaration that a signature is valid

15. Suppose you typed the original and three copies of a legal document which was dictated by an attorney in your office. He has already signed the original copy, and corrections have been made on all copies.   15.____
Regarding the copies, which one of the following procedures is the PROPER one to follow?

    A. Leave the signature line blank on the copies
    B. Ask the attorney to sign the copies
    C. Print or type the attorney's name on the signature line on the copies
    D. Sign your name to the copies followed by the attorney's initials

16. Suppose your office is defending a particular person in a court action. This person comes to the office and asks to see some of the lawyer's working papers in his file. The lawyer assigned to the case is out of the office at the time.   16.____
You SHOULD

    A. permit him to examine his entire file as long as he does not remove any materials from it
    B. make an appointment for the caller to come back later when the lawyer will be there
    C. ask him what working papers he wants to see and show him only those papers
    D. tell him that he needs written permission from the lawyer in order to see any records

17. Suppose that you receive a phone call from an official who is annoyed about a letter from your office which she just received. The lawyer who dictated the letter is not in the office at the moment.
Of the following, the BEST action for you to take is to

    A. explain that the lawyer is out but that you will ask the lawyer to return her call when he returns
    B. take down all of the details of her complaint and tell her that you will get back to her with an explanation
    C. refer to the proper file so that you can give her an explanation of the reasons for the letter over the phone
    D. make an appointment for her to stop by the office to speak with the lawyer

17.____

18. Suppose that you have taken dictation for an interoffice memorandum. You are asked to prepare it for distribution to four lawyers in your department whose names are given to you. You will type an original and make four copies. Which one of the following is COR-RECT with regard to the typing of the lawyers' names?
The names of all of the lawyers should appear

    A. *only* on the original
    B. on the original and each copy should have the name of one lawyer
    C. on each of the copies but not on the original
    D. on the original and on all of the copies

18.____

19. Regarding the correct typing of punctuation, the GENERALLY accepted practice is that there should be

    A. two spaces after a semi-colon
    B. one space before an apostrophe used in the body of a word
    C. no space between parentheses and the matter enclosed
    D. one space before and after a hyphen

19.____

20. Suppose you have just completed typing an original and two copies of a letter requesting information. The original is to be signed by a lawyer in your office. The first copy is for the files, and the second is to be used as a reminder to follow up.
The PROPER time to file the file copy of the letter is

    A. after the letter has been signed and corrections have been made on the copies
    B. before you take the letter to the lawyer for his signature
    C. after a follow-up letter has been sent
    D. after a response to the letter has been received

20.____

21. A secretary in a legal office has just typed a letter. She has typed the copy distribution notation on the copies to indicate *blind copy distribution*. This *blind copy* notation shows that

    A. copies of the letter are being sent to persons that the addressee does not know
    B. copies of the letter are being sent to other persons without the addressee's knowledge
    C. a copy of the letter will be enlarged for a legally blind person
    D. a copy of the letter is being given as an extra copy to the addressee

21.____

22. Suppose that one of the attorneys in your office dictates material to you without indicating punctuation. He has asked that you give him, as soon as possible, a single copy of a rough draft to be triple-spaced so that he can make corrections.
Of the following, what is the BEST thing for you to do in this situation?

    A. Assume that no punctuation is desired in the material
    B. Insert the punctuation as you type the rough draft
    C. Transcribe the material exactly as dictated, but attach a note to the attorney stating your suggested changes
    D. Before you start to type the draft, tell the attorney you want to read back your notes so that he can indicate punctuation

22.____

23. When it is necessary to type a mailing notation such as CERTIFIED, REGISTERED, or FEDEX on an envelope, the GENERALLY accepted place to type it is

    A. directly above the address
    B. in the area below where the stamp will be affixed
    C. in the lower left-hand corner
    D. in the upper left-hand corner

23.____

24. When taking a citation of a case in shorthand, which of the following should you write FIRST if you are having difficulty keeping up with the dictation?

    A. Volume and page number   B. Title of volume
    C. Name of plaintiff   D. Name of defendant

24.____

25. All of the following abbreviations and their meanings are correctly paired EXCEPT

    A. viz. - namely   B. ibid. - refer
    C. n.b. - note well   D. q.v. - which see

25.____

KEY (CORRECT ANSWERS)

1.	D		11.	D
2.	D		12.	A
3.	B		13.	B
4.	B		14.	D
5.	A		15.	C
6.	C		16.	B
7.	D		17.	A
8.	A		18.	D
9.	A		19.	C
10.	C		20.	A

21.	B
22.	B
23.	B
24.	A
25.	B

EXAMINATION SECTION
TEST 1

DIRECTIONS: Each question or incomplete statement is followed by several suggested
answers or completions. Select the one that BEST answers the question or
completes the statement. *PRINT THE LETTER OF THE CORRECT ANSWER
IN THE SPACE AT THE RIGHT.*

1. Assume that a few co-workers meet near your desk and talk about personal matters dur-   1.____
    ing working hours. Lately, this practice has interfered with your work.
    In order to stop this practice, the BEST action for you to take FIRST is to

    A.   ask your supervisor to put a stop to the co-workers' meeting near your desk
    B.   discontinue any friendship with this group
    C.   ask your co-workers not to meet near your desk
    D.   request that your desk be moved to another location

2. In order to maintain office coverage during working hours, your supervisor has scheduled   2.____
    your lunch hour from 1 P.M. to 2 P.M. and your co-worker's lunch hour from 12 P.M. to 1
    P.M. Lately, your co-worker has been returning late from lunch each day. As a result, you
    don't get a full hour since you must return to the office by 2 P.M.
    Of the following, the BEST action for you to take FIRST is to

    A.   explain to your co-worker in a courteous manner that his lateness is interfering with
         your right to a full hour for lunch
    B.   tell your co-worker that his lateness must stop or you will report him to your super-
         visor
    C.   report your co-worker's lateness to your supervisor
    D.   leave at 1 P.M. for lunch, whether your co-worker has returned or not

3. Assume that, as an office worker, one of your jobs is to open mail sent to your unit, read   3.____
    the mail for content, and send the mail to the appropriate person to handle. You acciden-
    tally open and begin to read a letter marked *personal* addressed to a co-worker.
    Of the following, the BEST action for you to take is to

    A.   report to your supervisor that your co-worker is receiving personal mail at the office
    B.   destroy the letter so that your co-worker does not know you saw it
    C.   reseal the letter and place it on the co-worker's desk without saying anything
    D.   bring the letter to your co-worker and explain that you opened it by accident

4. Suppose that in evaluating your work, your supervisor gives you an overall good rating,   4.____
    but states that you sometimes turn in work with careless errors.
    The BEST action for you to take would be to

    A.   ask a co-worker who is good at details to proofread your work
    B.   take time to do a careful job, paying more attention to detail
    C.   continue working as usual since occasional errors are to be expected
    D.   ask your supervisor if she would mind correcting your errors

5. Assume that you are taking a telephone message for a co-worker who is not in the office   5.____
    at the time.
    Of the following, the LEAST important item to write on the message is the

    A.   length of the call   B.   name of the caller
    C.   time of the call   D.   telephone number of the caller

Questions 6-13.

DIRECTIONS: Questions 6 through 13 each consist of a sentence which may or may not be an example of good English. The underlined parts of each sentence may be correct or incorrect. Examine each sentence, considering grammar, punctuation, spelling, and capitalization. If the English usage in the underlined parts of the sentence given is better than any of the changes in the underlined words suggested in Options B, C, or D, choose Option A. If the changes in the underlined words suggested in Options B, C, or D would make the sentence correct, choose the correct option. Do not choose an option that will change the meaning of the sentence.

6.   This <u>Fall</u>, the office will be closed on <u>Columbus Day, October</u> 9th.   6.____

    A.   Correct as is
    B.   fall...Columbus Day, October
    C.   Fall...columbus day, October
    D.   fall...Columbus Day, october

7.   This manual <u>discribes the duties performed</u> by an Office Aide.   7.____

    A.   Correct as is
    B.   describe the duties performed
    C.   discribe the duties performed
    D.   describes the duties performed

8.   There <u>weren't no</u> paper in the supply closet.   8.____

    A.   Correct as is   B.   weren't any
    C.   wasn't any   D.   wasn't no

9.   The new employees left <u>there</u> office to attend a meeting.   9.____

    A.   Correct as is   B.   they're
    C.   their   D.   thier

10.   The office worker started working at <u>8:30 a.m.</u>   10.____

    A.   Correct as is   B.   8:30 a.m.
    C.   8;30 a,m.   D.   8:30 am.

11.   The <u>alphabet, or A to Z sequence</u> are the basis of most filing systems.   11.____

    A.   Correct as is
    B.   alphabet, or A to Z sequence, is
    C.   alphabet, or A to Z sequence are
    D.   alphabet, or A too Z sequence, is

12.   <u>Those</u> file cabinets are five <u>feet</u> tall.   12.____

    A.   Correct as is   B.   Them...feet
    C.   Those...foot   D.   Them...foot

13. The Office Aide checked the <u>register and finding</u> the date of the meeting.   13._____

    A. Correct as is   B. regaster and finding
    C. register and found   D. regaster and found

Questions 14-21.

DIRECTIONS: Each of Questions 14 through 21 has two lists of numbers. Each list contains three sets of numbers. Check each of the three sets in the list on the right to see if they are the same as the corresponding set in the list on the left. Mark your answers:

    A.   If none of the sets in the right list are the same as those in the left list
    B.   if only one of the sets in the right list are the same as those in the left list
    C.   if only two of the sets in the right list are the same as those in the left list
    D.   if all three sets in the right list are the same as those in the left list

14. 7354183476   7354983476   14._____
      4474747744   4474747774
      57914302311   57914302311

15. 7143592185   7143892185   15._____
      8344517699   8344518699
      9178531263   9178531263

16. 2572114731   257214731   16._____
      8806835476   8806835476
      8255831246   8255831246

17. 331476853821   331476858621   17._____
      6976658532996   6976655832996
      3766042113715   3766042113745

18. 8806663315   8806663315   18._____
      74477138449   74477138449
      211756663666   211756663666

19. 990006966996   99000696996   19._____
      53022219743   53022219843
      4171171117717   4171171177717

20. 24400222433004   24400222433004   20._____
      5300030055000355   5300030055500355
      20000075532002022   20000075532002022

21. 6111666406600001116   6111666406600001116   21._____
      7111300117001100733   7111300117001100733
      26666446664476518   26666446664476518

Questions 22-25.

DIRECTIONS: Each of Questions 22 through 25 has two lists of names and addresses. Each list contains three sets of names and addresses. Check each of the three sets in the list on the right to see if they are the same as the corresponding set in the list on the left. Mark your answers:

- A. if none of the sets in the right list are the same as those in the left list
- B. if only one of the sets in the right list is the same as those in the left list
- C. if only two of the sets in the right list are the same as those in the left list
- D. if all three sets in the right list are the same as those in the left list

22. Mary T. Berlinger
2351 Hampton St.
Monsey, N.Y. 20117

    Eduardo Benes
    473 Kingston Avenue
    Central Islip, N.Y. 11734

    Alan Carrington Fuchs
    17 Gnarled Hollow Road
    Los Angeles, CA 91635

    Mary T. Berlinger
    2351 Hampton St.
    Monsey, N.Y. 20117

    Eduardo Benes
    473 Kingston Avenue
    Central Islip, N.Y. 11734

    Alan Carrington Fuchs
    17 Gnarled Hollow Road
    Los Angeles, CA 91685

22._____

23. David John Jacobson
178 35 St. Apt. 4C
New York, N.Y. 00927

    Ann-Marie Calonella
    7243 South Ridge Blvd.
    Bakersfield, CA 96714

    Pauline M. Thompson
    872 Linden Ave.
    Houston, Texas 70321

    David John Jacobson
    178 53 St. Apt. 4C
    New York, N.Y. 00927

    Ann-Marie Calonella
    7243 South Ridge Blvd.
    Bakersfield, CA 96714

    Pauline M. Thomson
    872 Linden Ave.
    Houston, Texas 70321

23._____

24. Chester LeRoy Masterton
152 Lacy Rd.
Kankakee, Ill. 54532

    William Maloney
    S. LaCrosse Pla.
    Wausau, Wisconsin 52146

    Cynthia V. Barnes
    16 Pines Rd.
    Greenpoint, Miss. 20376

    Chester LeRoy Masterson
    152 Lacy Rd.
    Kankakee, Ill. 54532

    William Maloney
    S. LaCross Pla.
    Wausau, Wisconsin 52146

    Cynthia V. Barnes
    16 Pines Rd.
    Greenpoint, Miss. 20376

24._____

25. Marcel Jean Frontenac
6 Burton On The Water
Calender, Me. 01471

J. Scott Marsden
174 S. Tipton St.
Cleveland, Ohio

Lawrence T. Haney
171 McDonough St.
Decatur, Ga. 31304

Marcel Jean Frontenac
6 Burton On The Water
Calender, Me. 01471

J. Scott Marsden
174 Tipton St.
Cleveland, Ohio

Lawrence T. Haney
171 McDonough St.
Decatur, Ga. 31304

25._____

KEY (CORRECT ANSWERS)

1.	C		11.	B
2.	A		12.	A
3.	D		13.	C
4.	B		14.	B
5.	A		15.	B
6.	A		16.	C
7.	D		17.	A
8.	C		18.	D
9.	C		19.	A
10.	B		20.	C

21.	C
22.	C
23.	B
24.	B
25.	C

TEST 2

DIRECTIONS: Each question or incomplete statement is followed by several suggested answers or completions. Select the one that BEST answers the question or completes the statement. *PRINT THE LETTER OF THE CORRECT ANSWER IN THE SPACE AT THE RIGHT.*

Questions 1-6.

DIRECTIONS: Questions 1 through 6 are to be answered SOLELY on the basis of the information contained in the following passage.

Duplicating is the process of making a number of identical copies of letters, documents, etc. from an original. Some duplicating processes make copies directly from the original document. Other duplicating processes require the preparation of a special master, and copies are then made from the master. Four of the most common duplicating processes are stencil, fluid, offset, and xerox.

In the stencil process, the typewriter is used to cut the words into a master called a stencil. Drawings, charts, or graphs can be cut into the stencil using a stylus. As many as 3,500 good-quality copies can be reproduced from one stencil. Various grades of finished paper from inexpensive mimeograph to expensive bond can be used.

The fluid process is a good method of copying from 50 to 125 good-quality copies from a master, which is prepared with a special dye. The master is placed on the duplicator, and special paper with a hard finish is moistened and then passed through the duplicator. Some of the dye on the master is dissolved, creating an impression on the paper. The impression becomes lighter as more copies are made; and once the dye on the master is used up, a new master must be made.

The offset process is the most adaptable office duplicating process because this process can be used for making a few copies or many copies. Masters can be made on paper or plastic for a few hundred copies, or on metal plates for as many as 75,000 copies. By using a special technique called photo-offset, charts, photographs, illustrations, or graphs can be reproduced on the master plate. The offset process is capable of producing large quantities of fine, top-quality copies on all types of finished paper.

The xerox process reproduces an exact duplicate from an original. It is the fastest duplicating method because the original material is placed directly on the duplicator, eliminating the need to make a special master. Any kind of paper can be used. The xerox process is the most expensive duplicating process; however, it is the best method of reproducing small quantities of good-quality copies of reports, letters, official documents, memos, or contracts.

1. Of the following, the MOST efficient method of reproducing 5,000 copies of a graph is   1.____

    A. stencil   B. fluid   C. offset   D. xerox

2. The offset process is the MOST adaptable office duplicating process because   2.____

    A. it is the quickest duplicating method
    B. it is the least expensive duplicating method
    C. it can produce a small number or large number of copies
    D. a softer master can be used over and over again

3. Which one of the following duplicating processes uses moistened paper?   3.____

    A.   Stencil   B.   Fluid   C.   Offset   D.   Xerox

4. The fluid process would be the BEST process to use for reproducing   4.____

    A.   five copies of a school transcript
    B.   fifty copies of a memo
    C.   five hundred copies of a form letter
    D.   five thousand copies of a chart

5. Which one of the following duplicating processes does NOT require a special master?   5.____

    A.   Fluid   B.   Xerox   C.   Offset   D.   Stencil

6. Xerox is NOT used for all duplicating jobs because   6.____

    A.   it produces poor-quality copies
    B.   the process is too expensive
    C.   preparing the master is too time-consuming
    D.   it cannot produce written reports

7. Assume a city agency has 775 office workers.   7.____
If 2 out of 25 office workers were absent on a particular day, how many office workers reported to work on that day?

    A.   713   B.   744   C.   750   D.   773

Questions 8-11.

DIRECTIONS: In Questions 8 through 11, select the choice that is CLOSEST in meaning to the underlined word.

SAMPLE: This division reviews the fiscal reports of the agency.
            In this sentence, the word fiscal means MOST NEARLY
                A.   financial   B.   critical   C.   basic   D.   personnel

        The correct answer is A, financial, because financial is closest to fiscal.

8. A central file eliminates the need to retain duplicate material.   8.____
The word retain means MOST NEARLY

    A.   keep   B.   change   C.   locate   D.   process

9. Filing is a routine office task.   9.____
Routine means MOST NEARLY

    A.   proper   B.   regular   C.   simple   D.   difficult

10. Sometimes a word, phrase, or sentence must be deleted to correct an error.   10.____
Deleted means MOST NEARLY

    A.   removed   B.   added   C.   expanded   D.   improved

11. Your supervisor will <u>evaluate</u> your work.
    <u>Evaluate</u> means MOST NEARLY   11._____

    A. judge   B. list   C. assign   D. explain

Questions 12-19.

DIRECTIONS: The code table below shows 10 letters with matching numbers. For each Question 12 through 19, there are three sets of letters. Each set of letters is followed by a set of numbers which may or may not match their correct letter according to the code table. For each question, check all three sets of letters and numbers and mark your answer:
           A. if no pairs are correctly matched
           B. if only one pair is correctly matched
           C. if only two pairs are correctly matched
           D. if all three pairs are correctly matched

<u>CODE TABLE</u>

T	M	V	D	S	P	R	G	B	H
1	2	3	4	5	6	7	8	9	0

Sample Question: TMVDSP - 123456
                         RGBHTM - 789011
                         DSPRGB - 256789

In the sample question above, the first set of numbers correctly matches its set of letters. But the second and third pairs contain mistakes. In the second pair, M is incorrectly matched with number 1. According to the code table, letter M should be correctly matched with number 2. In the third pair, the letter D is incorrectly matched with number 2. According to the code table, letter D should be correctly matched with number 4. Since only one of the pairs is correctly matched, the answer to this sample question is B.

12. RSBMRM -   759262   12._____
      GDSRVH -   845730
      VDBRTM -   349713

13. TGVSDR -   183247   13._____
      SMHRDP -   520647
      TRMHSR -   172057

14. DSPRGM -   456782   14._____
      MVDBHT -   234902
      HPMDBT -   062491

15. BVPTRD -   936184   15._____
      GDPHMB -   807029
      GMRHMV -   827032

16. MGVRSH -   283750   16._____
      TRDMBS -   174295
      SPRMGV -   567283

17.	SGBSDM	-	489542
	MGHPTM	-	290612
	MPBMHT	-	269301

17.____

18.	TDPBHM	-	146902
	VPBMRS	-	369275
	GDMBHM	-	842902

18.____

19.	MVPTBV	-	236194
	PDRTMB	-	647128
	BGTMSM	-	981232

19.____

Questions 20-25.

DIRECTIONS: In each of Questions 20 through 25, the names of four people are given. For each question, choose as your answer the one of the four names given which should be filed FIRST according to the usual system of alphabetical filing of names, as described in the following paragraph.

In filing names, you must start with the last name. Names are filed in order of the first letter of the last name, then the second letter, etc. Therefore, BAILY would be filed before BROWN, which would be filed before COLT. A name with fewer letters of the same type comes first; i.e., Smith before Smithe. If the last names are the same, the names are filed alphabetically by the first name. If the first name is an initial, a name with an initial would come before a first name that starts with the same letter as the initial. Therefore, I. BROWN would come before IRA BROWN. Finally, if both last name and first name are the same, the name would be filed alphabetically by the middle name, one again an initial coming before a middle name which starts with the same letter as the initial. If there is no middle name at all, the name would come before those with middle initials or names.

Sample Question: A. Lester Daniels
                     B. William Dancer
                     C. Nathan Danzig
                     D. Dan Lester

The last names beginning with D are filed before the last name beginning with L. Since DANIELS, DANCER, and DANZIG all begin with the same three letters, you must look at the fourth letter of the last name to determine which name should be filed first. C comes before I or Z in the alphabet, so DANCER is filed before DANIELS or DANZIG. Therefore, the answer to the above sample question is B.

20.	A.	Scott Biala	B.	Mary Byala	20.____
	C.	Martin Baylor	D.	Francis Bauer	

21.	A.	Howard J. Black	B.	Howard Black	21.____
	C.	J. Howard Black	D.	John H. Black	

22.	A.	Theodora Garth Kingston	B.	Theadore Barth Kingston	22.____
	C.	Thomas Kingston	D.	Thomas T. Kingston	

23.	A.	Paulette Mary Huerta	B.	Paul M. Huerta	23.____
	C.	Paulette L. Huerta	D.	Peter A. Huerta	

24.　A.　Martha Hunt Morgan　　　　B.　Martin Hunt Morgan　　　　24.____
　　 C.　Mary H. Morgan　　　　　　　D.　Martine H. Morgan

25.　A.　James T. Meerschaum　　　　B.　James M. Mershum　　　　25.____
　　 C.　James F. Mearshaum　　　　　D.　James N. Meshum

KEY (CORRECT ANSWERS)

1.	C	11.	A
2.	C	12.	B
3.	B	13.	B
4.	B	14.	C
5.	B	15.	A
6.	B	16.	D
7.	A	17.	A
8.	A	18.	D
9.	B	19.	A
10.	A	20.	D

21.	B
22.	B
23.	B
24.	A
25.	C

TEST 3

DIRECTIONS: Each question or incomplete statement is followed by several suggested answers or completions. Select the one that BEST answers the question or completes the statement. *PRINT THE LETTER OF THE CORRECT ANSWER IN THE SPACE AT THE RIGHT.*

1. Which one of the following statements about proper telephone usage is NOT always correct?
   When answering the telephone, you should

   A. know whom you are speaking to
   B. give the caller your undivided attention
   C. identify yourself to the caller
   D. obtain the information the caller wishes before you do your other work

   1._____

2. Assume that, as a member of a worker's safety committee in your agency, you are responsible for encouraging other employees to follow correct safety practices. While you are working on your regular assignment, you observe an employee violating a safety rule.
   Of the following, the BEST action for you to take FIRST is to

   A. speak to the employee about safety practices and order him to stop violating the safety rule
   B. speak to the employee about safety practices and point out the safety rule he is violating
   C. bring the matter up in the next committee meeting
   D. report this violation of the safety rule to the employee's supervisor

   2._____

3. Assume that you have been temporarily assigned by your supervisor to do a job which you do not want to do. The BEST action for you to take is to

   A. discuss the job with your supervisor, explaining why you do not want to do it
   B. discuss the job with your supervisor and tell her that you will not do it
   C. ask a co-worker to take your place on this job
   D. do some other job that you like; your supervisor may give the job you do not like to someone else

   3._____

4. Assume that you keep the confidential personnel files of employees in your unit. A friend asks you to obtain some information from the file of one of your co-workers.
   The BEST action to take is to _____ to your friend.

   A. ask the co-worker if you can give the information
   B. ask your supervisor if you can give the information
   C. give the information
   D. refuse to give the information

   4._____

Questions 5-8.

DIRECTIONS: Questions 5 through 8 are to be answered SOLELY on the basis of the information contained in the following passage.

City government is committed to providing a safe and healthy work environment for all city employees. An effective agency safety program reduces accidents by educating employees about the types of careless acts which can cause accidents. Even in an office, accidents can happen. If each employee is aware of possible safety hazards, the number of accidents on the job can be reduced.

Careless use of office equipment can cause accidents and injuries. For example, file cabinet drawers which are filled with papers can be so heavy that the entire cabinet could tip over from the weight of one open drawer.

The bottom drawers of desks and file cabinets should never be left open since employees could easily trip over open drawers and injure themselves.

When reaching for objects on a high shelf, an employee should use a strong, sturdy object such as a step stool to stand on. Makeshift platforms made out of books, papers, or boxes can easily collapse. Even chairs can slide out from under foot, causing serious injury.

Even at an employee's desk, safety hazards can occur. Frayed or cut wires should be repaired or replaced immediately. Computers which are not firmly anchored to the desk or table could fall, causing injury.

Smoking is one of the major causes of fires in the office. A lighted match or improperly extinguished cigarette thrown into a wastebasket filled with paper could cause a major fire with possible loss of life. Where smoking is permitted, ashtrays should be used. Smoking is particularly dangerous in offices where flammable chemicals are used.

5. The goal of an effective safety program is to   5.____

    A. reduce office accidents
    B. stop employees from smoking on the job
    C. encourage employees to continue their education
    D. eliminate high shelves in offices

6. Desks and file cabinets can become safety hazards when   6.____

    A. their drawers are left open
    B. they are used as wastebaskets
    C. they are makeshift
    D. they are not anchored securely to the floor

7. Smoking is especially hazardous when it occurs   7.____

    A. near exposed wires
    B. in a crowded office
    C. in an area where flammable chemicals are used
    D. where books and papers are stored

8. Accidents are likely to occur when   8.____

    A. employees' desks are cluttered with books and papers
    B. employees are not aware of safety hazards
    C. employees close desk drawers
    D. step stools are used to reach high objects

9. Assume that part of your job as a worker in the accounting division of a city agency is to answer the telephone. When you first answer the telephone, it is LEAST important to tell the caller

    A. your title   B. your name
    C. the name of your unit   D. the name of your agency

9.____

10. Assume that you are assigned to work as a receptionist, and your duties are to answer phones, greet visitors, and do other general office work. You are busy with a routine job when several visitors approach your desk.
The BEST action to take is to

    A. ask the visitors to have a seat and assist them after your work is completed
    B. tell the visitors that you are busy and they should return at a more convenient time
    C. stop working long enough to assist the visitors
    D. continue working and wait for the visitors to ask you for assistance

10.____

11. Assume that your supervisor has chosen you to take a special course during working hours to learn a new payroll procedure. Although you know that you were chosen because of your good work record, a co-worker, who feels that he should have been chosen, has been telling everyone in your unit that the choice was unfair.
Of the following, the BEST way to handle this situation FIRST is to

    A. suggest to the co-worker that everything in life is unfair
    B. contact your union representative in case your co-worker presents a formal grievance
    C. tell your supervisor about your co-worker's complaints and let her handle the situation
    D. tell the co-worker that you were chosen because of your superior work record

11.____

12. Assume that while you are working on an assignment which must be completed quickly, a supervisor from another unit asks you to obtain information for her.
Of the following, the BEST way to respond to her request is to

    A. tell her to return in an hour since you are busy
    B. give her the names of some people in her own unit who could help her
    C. tell her you are busy and refer her to a co-worker
    D. tell her that you are busy and ask her if she could wait until you finish your assignment

12.____

13. A co-worker in your unit is often off from work because of illness. Your supervisor assigns the co-worker's work to you when she is not there. Lately, doing her work has interfered with your own job.
The BEST action for you to take FIRST is to

    A. discuss the problem with your supervisor
    B. complete your own work before starting your co-worker's work
    C. ask other workers in your unit to assist you
    D. work late in order to get the jobs done

13.____

14. During the month of June, 40,587 people attended a city-owned swimming pool. In July, 13,014 more people attended the swimming pool than the number that had attended in June. In August, 39,655 people attended the swimming pool.
    The TOTAL number of people who attended the swimming pool during the months of June, July, and August was

14.____

    A. 80,242   B. 93,256   C. 133,843   D. 210,382

Questions 15-22.

DIRECTIONS: Questions 15 through 22 test how well you understand what you read. It will be necessary for you to read carefully because your answers to these questions must be based ONLY on the information in the following paragraphs.

The telephone directory is made up of two books. The first book consists of the introductory section and the alphabetical listing of names section. The second book is the classified directory (also known as the yellow pages). Many people who are familiar with one book do not realize how useful the other can be. The efficient office worker should become familiar with both books in order to make the best use of this important source of information.

The introductory section gives general instructions for finding numbers in the alphabetical listing and classified directory. This section also explains how to use the telephone company's many services, including the operator and information services, gives examples of charges for local and long-distance calls, and lists area codes for the entire country. In addition, this section provides a useful postal zip code map.

The alphabetical listing of names section lists the names, addresses, and telephone numbers of subscribers in an area. Guide names, or *telltales,* are on the top corner of each page. These guide names indicate the first and last name to be found on that page. *Telltales* help locate any particular name quickly. A cross-reference spelling is also given to help locate names which are spelled several different ways. City, state, and federal government agencies are listed under the major government heading. For example, an agency of the federal government would be listed under *United States Government.*

The classified directory, or yellow pages, is a separate book. In this section are advertising services, public transportation line maps, shopping guides, and listings of businesses arranged by the type of product or services they offer. This book is most useful when looking for the name or phone number of a business when all that is known is the type of product offered and the address, or when trying to locate a particular type of business in an area. Businesses listed in the classified directory can usually be found in the alphabetical listing of names section. When the name of the business is known, you will find the address or phone number more quickly in the alphabetical listing of names section.

15.   The introductory section provides

15.____

    A. shopping guides   B. government listings
    C. business listings   D. information services

16.   Advertising services would be found in the

16.____

    A. introductory section   B. alphabetical listing of names section
    C. classified directory   D. information services

17. According to the information in the above passage for locating government agencies, the Information Office of the Department of Consumer Affairs of New York City government would be alphabetically listed FIRST under

    A. *I* for Information Offices
    B. *D* for Department of Consumer Affairs
    C. *N* for New York City
    D. *G* for government

17._____

18. When the name of a business is known, the QUICKEST way to find the phone number is to look in the

    A. classified directory
    B. introductory section
    C. alphabetical listing of names section
    D. advertising service section

18.____

19. The QUICKEST way to find the phone number of a business when the type of service a business offers and its address is known is to look in the

    A. classified directory
    B. alphabetical listing of names section
    C. introductory section
    D. information service

19.____

20. What is a *telltale?*

    A. An alphabetical listing
    B. A guide name
    C. A map
    D. A cross-reference listing

20.____

21. The BEST way to find a postal zip code is to look in the

    A. classified directory
    B. introductory section
    C. alphabetical listing of names section
    D. government heading

21.____

22. To help find names which have several different spellings, the telephone directory provides

    A. cross-reference spelling   B. *telltales*
    C. spelling guides   D. advertising services

22.____

23. Assume that your agency has been given $2025 to purchase file cabinets. If each file cabinet costs $135, how many file cabinets can your agency purchase?

    A. 8   B. 10   C. 15   D. 16

23.____

24. Assume that your unit ordered 14 staplers at a total cost of $30.20, and each stapler cost the same.
The cost of one stapler was MOST NEARLY

    A. $1.02   B. $1.61   C. $2.16   D. $2.26

24.____

25. Assume that you are responsible for counting and recording licensing fees collected by your department. On a particular day, your department collected in fees 40 checks in the amount of $6 each, 80 checks in the amount of $4 each, 45 twenty dollar bills, 30 ten dollar bills, 42 five dollar bills, and 186 one dollar bills.
The TOTAL amount in fees collected on that day was

    A. $1,406   B. $1,706   C. $2,156   D. $2,356

25.____

26. Assume that you are responsible for your agency's petty cash fund. During the month of February, you pay out 7 $2.00 subway fares and one taxi fare for $10.85. You pay out nothing else from the fund. At the end of February, you count the money left in the fund and find 3 one dollar bills, 4 quarters, 5 dimes, and 4 nickels. The amount of money you had available in the petty cash fund at the BEGINNING of February was

    A. $4.70   B. $16.35   C. $24.85   D. $29.55

26.____

27. You overhear your supervisor criticize a co-worker for handling equipment in an unsafe way. You feel that the criticism may be unfair.
Of the following, it would be BEST for you to

    A. take your co-worker aside and tell her how you feel about your supervisor's comments
    B. interrupt the discussion and defend your co-worker to your supervisor
    C. continue working as if you had not overheard the discussion
    D. make a list of other workers who have violated safety rules and give it to your supervisor

27.____

28. Assume that you have been assigned to work on a long-term project with an employee who is known for being uncooperative.
In beginning to work with this employee, it would be LEAST desirable for you to

    A. understand why the person is uncooperative
    B. act in a calm manner rather than an emotional manner
    C. be appreciative of the co-worker's work
    D. report the co-worker's lack of cooperation to your supervisor

28.____

29. Assume that you are assigned to sell tickets at a city-owned ice skating rink. An adult ticket costs $4.50, and a children's ticket costs $2.25. At the end of a day, you find that you have sold 36 adult tickets and 80 children's tickets.
The TOTAL amount of money you collected for that day was

    A. $244.80   B. $318.00   C. $342.00   D. $348.00

29.____

30. If each office worker files 487 index cards in one hour, how many cards can 26 office workers file in one hour?

    A. 10,662   B. 12,175   C. 12,662   D. 14,266

30.____

KEY (CORRECT ANSWERS)

1.	D	16.	C
2.	B	17.	C
3.	A	18.	C
4.	D	19.	A
5.	A	20.	B
6.	A	21.	B
7.	C	22.	A
8.	B	23.	C
9.	A	24.	C
10.	C	25.	C
11.	C	26.	D
12.	D	27.	C
13.	A	28.	D
14.	C	29.	C
15.	D	30.	C

EXAMINATION SECTION
TEST 1

DIRECTIONS: Each question or incomplete statement is followed by several suggested answers or completions. Select the one that BEST answers the question or completes the statement. *PRINT THE LETTER OF THE CORRECT ANSWER IN THE SPACE AT THE RIGHT.*

1. If you open a personal letter by mistake, the one of the following actions which it would generally be BEST for you to take is to   1.____

    A. ignore your error, attach the envelope to the letter, and distribute in the usual manner
    B. personally give the addressee the letter without any explanation
    C. place the letter inside the envelope, indicate under your initials that it was opened in error, and give to the addressee
    D. reseal the envelope or place the contents in another envelope and pass on to addressee

2. If you receive a telephone call regarding a matter which your office does not handle, you should FIRST   2.____

    A. give the caller the telephone number of the proper office so that he can dial again
    B. offer to transfer the caller to the proper office
    C. suggest that the caller re-dial since he probably dialed incorrectly
    D. tell the caller he has reached the wrong office and then hang up

3. When you answer the telephone, the MOST important reason for identifying yourself and your organization is to   3.____

    A. give the caller time to collect his or her thoughts
    B. impress the caller with your courtesy
    C. inform the caller that he or she has reached the right number
    D. set a business-like tone at the beginning of the conversation

4. The one of the following cases in which you would NOT place a special notation in the left margin of a letter that you have typed is when   4.____

    A. one of the copies is intended for someone other than the addressee of the letter
    B. you enclose a flyer with the letter
    C. you sign your superior's name to the letter, at his or her request
    D. the letter refers to something being sent under separate cover

5. Suppose that you accidentally cut a letter or enclosure as you are opening an envelope with a paper knife.
The one of the following that you should do FIRST is to   5.____

    A. determine whether the document is important
    B. clip or staple the pieces together and process as usual
    C. mend the cut document with transparent tape
    D. notify the sender that the communication was damaged and request another copy

6. As soon as you pick up the phone, a very angry caller begins immediately to complain about city agencies and *red tape*. He says that he has been shifted to two or three different offices. It turns out that he is seeking information which is not immediately available to you. You believe you know, however, where it can be found.
Which of the following actions is the BEST one for you to take?

    A. To eliminate all confusion, suggest that the caller write the mayor stating explicitly what he wants.
    B. Apologize by telling the caller how busy city agencies now are, but also tell him directly that you do not have the information he needs.
    C. Ask for the caller's telephone number, and assure him you will call back after you have checked further.
    D. Give the caller the name and telephone number of the person who might be able to help, but explain that you are not positive he will get results.

6.____

7. Suppose that one of your duties is to dictate responses to routine requests from the public for information. A letter writer asks for information which, as expressed in a one-sentence, explicit agency rule, cannot be given out to the public.
Of the following ways of answering the letter, which is the MOST efficient?

    A. Quote verbatim that section of the agency rules which prohibits giving this information to the public.
    B. Without quoting the rule, explain why you cannot accede to the request and suggest alternative sources.
    C. Describe how carefully the request was considered before classifying it as subject to the rule forbidding the issuance of such information.
    D. Acknowledge receipt of the letter and advise that the requested information is not released to the public.

7.____

8. Suppose you assist in supervising a staff which has rather high morale, and your own supervisor asks you to poll the staff to find out who will be able to work overtime this particular evening to help complete emergency work.
Which of the following approaches would be MOST likely to win their cooperation while maintaining their morale?

    A. Tell them that the better assignments will be given only to those who work overtime.
    B. Tell them that occasional overtime is a job requirement.
    C. Assure them they'll be doing you a personal favor.
    D. Let them know clearly why the overtime is needed.

8.____

9. Suppose that you have been asked to write and to prepare for reproduction new departmental vacation leave regulations.
After you have written the new regulations, all of which fit on two pages, which one of the following would be the BEST method of reproducing 1,000 copies?

    A. An outside private printer because you can best maintain confidentiality using this technique
    B. Photocopying because the copies will have the best possible appearance
    C. Sending the file to all department employees as printable PDFs
    D. Printing and collating on the office high-volume printer

9.____

10. You are in charge of verifying employees' qualifications. This involves telephoning previ- 10.____
ous employers and schools. One of the applications which you are reviewing contains
information which you are almost certain is correct on the basis of what the employee
has told you.
The BEST thing to do is to

    A. check the information again with the employer
    B. perform the required verification procedures
    C. accept the information as valid
    D. ask a superior to verify the information

11. The practice of immediately identifying oneself and one's place of employment when 11.____
contacting persons on the telephone is

    A. *good* because the receiver of the call can quickly identify the caller and establish a
frame of reference
    B. *good* because it helps to set the caller at ease with the other party
    C. *poor* because it is not necessary to divulge that information when making general
calls
    D. *poor* because it takes longer to arrive at the topic to be discussed

12. Which one of the following should be the MOST important overall consideration when 12.____
preparing a recommendation to automate a large-scale office activity?
The

    A. number of models of automated equipment available
    B. benefits and costs of automation
    C. fears and resistance of affected employees
    D. experience of offices which have automated similar activities

13. A tickler file is MOST appropriate for filing materials 13.____

    A. chronologically according to date they were received
    B. alphabetically by name
    C. alphabetically by subject
    D. chronologically according to date they should be followed up

14. Which of the following is the BEST reason for decentralizing rather then centralizing the 14.____
use of duplicating machines?

    A. Developing and retaining efficient duplicating machine operators
    B. Facilitating supervision of duplicating services
    C. Motivating employees to produce legible duplicated copies
    D. Placing the duplicating machines where they are most convenient and most fre-
quently used

15. Window envelopes are sometimes considered preferable to individually addressed enve- 15.____
lopes PRIMARILY because

    A. window envelopes are available in standard sizes for all purposes
    B. window envelopes are more attractive and official-looking
    C. the use of window envelopes eliminates the risk of inserting a letter in the wrong
envelope
    D. the use of window envelopes requires neater typing

16. In planning the layout of a new office, the utilization of space and the arrangement of staff, furnishings, and equipment should usually be MOST influenced by the

    A. gross square footage
    B. status differences in the chain of command
    C. framework of informal relationships among employees
    D. activities to be performed

16.____

17. Office forms sometimes consist of several copies, each of a different color. The MAIN reason for using different colors is to

    A. make a favorable impression on the users of the form
    B. distinguish each copy from the others
    C. facilitate the preparation of legible carbon copies
    D. reduce cost, since using colored stock permits recycling of paper

17.____

18. Which of the following is the BEST justification for obtaining a photocopying machine for the office?

    A. A photocopying machine can produce an unlimited number of copies at a low fixed cost per copy.
    B. Employees need little training in operating a photocopying machine.
    C. Office costs will be reduced and efficiency increased.
    D. The legibility of a photocopy generally is superior to copy produced by any other office duplicating device.

18.____

19. An administrative officer in charge of a small fund for buying office supplies has just written a check to Charles Laird, a supplier, and has sent the check by messenger to him. A half-hour later, the messenger telephones the administrative officer. He has lost the check.
Which of the following is the MOST important action for the administrative officer to take under these circumstances?

    A. Ask the messenger to return and write a report describing the loss of the check.
    B. Make a note on the performance record of the messenger who lost the check.
    C. Take the necessary steps to have payment stopped on the check.
    D. Refrain from doing anything since the check may be found shortly.

19.____

20. A petty cash fund is set up PRIMARILY to

    A. take care of small investments that must be made from time to time
    B. take care of small expenses that arise from time to time
    C. provide a fund to be used as the office wants to use it with little need to maintain records
    D. take care of expenses that develop during emergencies such as machine breakdowns and fires

20.____

21. Your superior has asked you to send a package from your agency to a government agency in another city. He has written out the message and has indicated the name of the government agency.
When you prepare the package for mailing, which of the following items that your superior has not mentioned must you be sure to include?

21.____

A. Today's date
B. The full address of the government agency
C. A polite opening such as *Dear Sirs*
D. A final sentence such as *We would appreciate hearing from your agency in reply as soon as is convenient for you*

22. In addition to the original piece of correspondence, one should USUALLY also have typed   22.____

    A. a single copy
    B. as many copies as can be typed at one time
    C. no more copies than are needed
    D. two copies

23. The one of the following which is the BEST procedure to follow when making a short insert in a completed dictation is to   23.____

    A. label the insert with a letter and indicate the position of the insert in the text by writing the identifying letter in the proper place
    B. squeeze the insert into its proper place within the main text of the dictation
    C. take down the insert and check the placement with the person who dictated when you are ready to transcribe your notes
    D. transcribe the dictation into longhand, including the insert in its proper position

24. The one of the following procedures which will be MOST efficient in helping you to quickly open your dictation notebook to a clean sheet is to   24.____

    A. clip or place a rubberband around the used portion of the notebook
    B. leave the book out and open to a clean page when not in use
    C. transcribe each dictation after it is given and rip out the used pages
    D. use a book marker to indicate which portion of the notebook has been used

25. The purpose of dating your dictation notebooks is GENERALLY to   25.____

    A. enable you to easily refer to your notes at a later date
    B. ensure that you transcribe your notes in the order in which they were dictated
    C. set up a precise record-keeping procedure
    D. show your employer that you pay attention to detail

——————

KEY (CORRECT ANSWERS)

1.	C		11.	A
2.	B		12.	B
3.	C		13.	D
4.	C		14.	D
5.	C		15.	C
6.	C		16.	D
7.	A		17.	B
8.	D		18.	C
9.	D		19.	C
10.	B		20.	B

21.	B
22.	C
23.	A
24.	A
25.	A

TEST 2

DIRECTIONS: Each question or incomplete statement is followed by several suggested answers or completions. Select the one that BEST answers the question or completes the statement. *PRINT THE LETTER OF THE CORRECT ANSWER IN THE SPACE AT THE RIGHT.*

1. With regard to typed correspondence received by most offices, which of the following is the GREATEST problem?

    A. Verbosity   B. Illegibility
    C. Improper folding   D. Excessive copies

1._____

2. Of the following, the GREATEST advantage of flash drives over rewritable CD storage is that they

    A. are portable
    B. are both smaller and lighter
    C. contain more storage space
    D. allow files to be deleted to free space

2._____

3. Suppose that a large quantity of information is in the files which are located a good distance from your desk. Almost every worker in your office must use these files constantly. Your duties in particular require that you daily refer to about 25 of the same items. They are short, one-page items distributed throughout the files. In this situation, your BEST course would be to

    A. take the items that you use daily from the files and keep them on your desk, inserting *out cards* in their place
    B. go to the files each time you need the information so that the items will be there when other workers need them
    C. make xerox copies of the information you use most frequently and keep them in your desk for ready reference
    D. label the items you use most often with different colored tabs for immediate identification

3._____

4. Of the following, the MOST important advantage of preparing manuals of office procedures in loose-leaf form is that this form

    A. permits several employees to use different sections simultaneously
    B. facilitates the addition of new material and the removal of obsolete material
    C. is more readily arranged in alphabetical order
    D. reduces the need for cross-references to locate material carried under several headings

4._____

5. Suppose that you establish a new clerical procedure for the unit you supervise. Your keeping a close check on the time required by your staff to handle the new procedure is WISE mainly because such a check will find out

    A. whether your subordinates know how to handle the new procedure
    B. whether a revision of the unit's work schedule will be necessary as a result of the new procedure
    C. what attitude your employees have toward the new procedure
    D. what alterations in job descriptions will be necessitated by the new procedure

5._____

6. The numbered statements below relate to the stenographic skill of taking dictation. According to authorities on secretarial practices, which of these are generally recommended guides to development of efficient stenographic skills?

STATEMENTS

1. A stenographer should date her notebook daily to facilitate locating certain notes at a later time.
2. A stenographer should make corrections of grammatical mistakes while her boss is dictating to her.
3. A stenographer should draw a line through the dictated matter in her notebook after she has transcribed it.
4. A stenographer should write in longhand unfamiliar names and addresses dictated to her.

The CORRECT answer is:

A. Only Statements 1, 2, and 3 are generally recommended guides.
B. Only Statements 2, 3, and 4 are generally recommended guides.
C. Only Statements 1, 3, and 4 are generally recommended guides.
D. All four statements are generally recommended guides.

7. According to generally recognized rules of filing in an alphabetic filing system, the one of the following names which normally should be filed LAST is

A. Department of Education, New York State
B. F.B.I.
C. Police Department of New York City
D. P.S. 81 of New York City

8. Which one of the following forms for the typed name of the dictator in the closing lines of a letter is generally MOST acceptable in the United States?

A. (Dr.) James F. Fenton
B. Dr. James F. Fenton
C. Mr. James F. Fenton, Ph.D.
D. James F. Fenton

9. Which of the following is, MOST generally, a rule to be followed when typing a rough draft?

A. The copy should be single spaced.
B. The copy should be triple spaced.
C. There is no need for including footnotes.
D. Errors must be neatly corrected.

10. An office assistant needs a synonym.
Of the following, the book which she would find MOST useful is

A. a world atlas
B. BARTLETT'S FAMILIAR QUOTATIONS
C. a manual of style
D. a thesaurus

11. Of the following examples of footnotes, the one that is expressed in the MOST generally accepted standard form is: 11._____

    A. Johnson, T.F. (Dr.), <u>English for Everyone</u>, 3rd or 4th edition; New York City Linton Publishing Company, p. 467

    B. Frank Taylor, <u>English for Today</u> (New York: Rayton Publishing Company, 1971), p. 156

    C. Ralph Wilden,<u> English for Tomorrow,</u> Reynolds Publishing Company, England, p. 451

    D. Quinn, David, Yesterday's English (New York: Baldwin Publishing Company, 1972), p. 431

12. Standard procedures are used in offices PRIMARILY because   12._____

    A. an office is a happier place if everyone is doing the tasks in the same manner

    B. particular ways of doing jobs are considered more efficient than other ways

    C. it is good discipline for workers to follow standard procedures approved by the supervisor

    D. supervisors generally don't want workers to be creative in planning their work

13. Assume that an office assistant has the responsibility for compiling, typing, and mailing a preliminary announcement of Spring term course offerings. The announcement will go to approximately 900 currently enrolled students. Assuming that the following equipment is available for use, the MOST EFFECTIVE method for distributing the announcement to all 900 students is to   13._____

    A. e-mail it as a text document using the electronic student mailing list

    B. post the announcement as a PDF document for download on the department website

    C. send it by fax

    D. post the announcement and leave copies in buildings around campus

14. *Justified typing* is a term that refers MOST specifically to typewriting copy   14._____

    A. that has been edited and for which final copy is being prepared

    B. in a form that allows for an even right-hand margin

    C. with a predetermined vertical placement for each alternate line

    D. that has been approved by the supervisor and his superior

15. Which one of the following is the BEST form for the address in a letter?   15._____

    A. Mr. John Jones
       Vice President, The Universal Printing Company
       1220 Fifth Avenue
       New York, 10023 New York

    B. Mr. John Jones, Vice President
       The Universal Printing Company
       1220 Fifth Avenue
       New York, New York 10023

    C. Mr. John Jones, Vice President, The Universal Printing Company
       1220 Fifth Avenue
       New York, New York 10023

D. Mr. John Jones Vice President,
The Universal Printing Company
1220 Fifth Avenue
New York, 10023 New York

16. Of the following, the CHIEF advantage of the use of window envelopes over ordinary
envelopes is that window envelopes

16.____

A. eliminate the need for addressing envelopes
B. protect the confidential nature of enclosed material
C. cost less to buy than ordinary envelopes
D. reduce the danger of the address becoming illegible

17. In the complimentary close of a business letter, the FIRST letter of _____ should be
capitalized.

17.____

A. all the words
C. only the first word
B. none of the words
D. only the last word

18. Assume that one of your duties is to procure needed office supplies from the supply
room. You are permitted to draw supplies every two weeks.
The one of the following which would be the MOST desirable practice for you to follow
in obtaining supplies is to

18.____

A. obtain a quantity of supplies sufficient to last for several months to make certain
that enough supplies are always on hand
B. determine the minimum supply necessary to keep on hand for the various items and
obtain an additional quantity as soon as possible after the supply on hand has been
reduced to this minimum
C. review the supplies once a month to determine what items have been exhausted
and obtain an additional quantity as soon as possible
D. obtain a supply of an item as soon after it has been exhausted as is possible

19. Some offices that keep carbon copies of letters use several different colors of carbon
paper for making carbon copies.
Of the following, the CHIEF reason for using different colors of carbon paper is to

19.____

A. facilitate identification of different types of letters in the files
B. relieve the monotony of typing and filing carbon copies
C. reduce the costs of preparing carbon copies
D. utilize both sides of the carbon paper for typing

20. Your supervisor asks you to post an online ad for freelance designers interested in
submitting samples for a new company logo. Prospective workers should be proficient in
which of the following software?

20.____

A. Microsoft Word
C. Adobe Illustrator
B. Adobe Acrobat Pro
D. Microsoft PowerPoint

21. Gary Thompson is applying for a position with the firm of Gray and Williams.
Which letter should be filed in top position in the *Application* folder?

21.____

A. A letter of recommendation written on September 18 by Johnson & Smith
B. Williams' letter of October 8 requesting further details regarding Thompson's experience

    C.   Thompson's letter of September 8 making application for a position as sales manager

    D.   Letter of September 20 from Alfred Jackson recommending Thompson for the job

22.   The USUAL arrangement in indexing the names of the First National Bank, Toledo, is   22.____

    A.   First National Bank, Toledo, Ohio
    B.   Ohio, First National Bank, Toledo
    C.   Toledo, First National Bank, Ohio
    D.   Ohio, Toledo, First National Bank

23.   A single line through typed text indicating that it's incorrect or invalid is known as a(n)   23.____

    A.   underline
    B.   strikethrough
    C.   line font
    D.   eraser

24.   A typical e-mail with an attachment should contain all of the following for successful transmittal EXCEPT   24.____

    A.   recipient's address   B.   file attachment
    C.   body text   D.   description of attachment

25.   The subject line in a letter is USUALLY typed a _____ space below the _____.   25.____

    A.   single; inside address   B.   single; salutation
    C.   double; inside address   D.   double; salutation

KEY (CORRECT ANSWERS)

1.	A		11.	B
2.	C		12.	B
3.	C		13.	A
4.	B		14.	B
5.	B		15.	B
6.	C		16.	A
7.	D		17.	C
8.	D		18.	B
9.	B		19.	A
10.	D		20.	C

21.	B
22.	A
23.	B
24.	D
25.	D

EXAMINATION SECTION

TEST 1

DIRECTIONS: Each question or incomplete statement is followed by several suggested answers or completions. Select the one that BEST answers the question or completes the statement. *PRINT THE LETTER OF THE CORRECT ANSWER IN THE SPACE AT THE RIGHT.*

1. The one of the following that is MOST advisable to do before transcribing your dictation notes is to
    A. check the syllabification of long words for typing purposes
    B. edit your notes
    C. number the pages of dictation
    D. sort them by the kind of typing format required

1._____

2. As a secretary, the one of the following which is LEAST important in writing a letter under your own signature is
    A. the accuracy of the information
    B. the appropriateness of the language
    C. the reason for the letter
    D. your supervisor's approval of the final copy

2._____

3. In a typed letter, the reference line is used
    A. for identification purposes on typed pages of more than one page
    B. to indicate under what heading the copy of the letter should be filed
    C. to indicate who dictated the letter and who typed it
    D. to make the subject of the letter prominent by typing it a single space below the salutation

3._____

Questions 4-5:

DIRECTIONS: For questions 4 and 5, choose the letter of the sentence that BEST and MOST clearly expresses its meaning.

4.   A. It has always been the practice of this office to effectuate recruitment of prospective employees from other departments.
    B. This office has always made a practice of recruiting prospective employees from other departments.
    C. Recruitment of prospective employees from other departments has always been a practice which has been implemented by this office.
    D. Implementation of the policy of recruitment of prospective employees from other departments has always been a practice of this office.

4._____

5.   A. These employees are assigned to the level of work evidenced by
         their efforts and skills during the training period.
      B. The level of work to which these employees is assigned is
         decided upon on the basis of the efforts and skills evidenced by
         them during the period in which they were trained.
      C. Assignment of these employees is made on the basis of the level
         of work their efforts and skills during the training period has
         evidenced.
      D. These employees are assigned to a level of work their efforts and
         skills during the training period have evidenced.

5._____

6. An office assistant was asked to mail a duplicated report of 100 pages to
   a professor in an out-of-town university. The professor sending the report
   dictated a short letter that he wanted to mail with the report.
   Of the following, the MOST inexpensive proper means of sending these
   two items would be to send the report
      A. and the letter first class
      B. by parcel post and the letter separately by air mail
      C. and the letter by parcel post
      D. by parcel post and attach to the package an envelope with first-
         class postage in which is enclosed the letter

6._____

7. Plans are underway to determine the productivity of the typists who work
   in a central office. Of the procedures listed, the one generally considered
   the MOST accurate for finding out the typists' output is to
      A. keep a record of how much typing is done over specified periods
         of time
      B. ask each typist how fast she types when she is doing a great deal
         of word processing
      C. give each typist a timed test during a specified period
      D. ask the supervisor to estimate the typing speed of each
         subordinate

7._____

8. Assume that an executive regularly receives the four types of mail listed
   below.
   As a general rule, the executive's secretary should arrange the mail from
   top to bottom so that the top items are
      A. advertisements
      B. airmail letters
      C. business letters
      D. unopened personal letters

8._____

9. An office assistant in transcribing reports and letters from dictation should   9._____
MOST generally assume that
    A. the transcript should be exactly what was dictated so there is little
need to check any details
    B. the dictated material is merely an idea of what the dictator wanted
to say so changes should be made to improve any part of the
dictation
    C. there may be some slight changes, but essentially the
transcription is to be a faithful copy of what was dictated
    D. the transcript is merely a very rough draft and should be typed
quickly so that the dictator can review it and make changes
preliminary to having the final copy typed

10. The one of the following which generally is the CHIEF disadvantage of   10._____
using office machines in place of human workers in office work is that the
machines are
    A. slower   B. less accurate
    C. more costly   D. less flexible

11. An office assistant in a New York City college is asked to place a call to a   11._____
prospective visiting professor in Los Angeles. It is 1 p.m. in New York
(EST). The time in Los Angeles is
    A. 9 a.m.   B. 10 a.m.   C. 4 p.m.   D. 5 p.m.

12. An office assistant is instructed to send a copy of a report to a professor   12._____
located in a building across campus. The fastest and most efficient way
for this report to reach the professor is by
    A. sending a messenger to hand-deliver it to the professor's office
    B. sending it via fax to the main office of the professor's department
    C. e-mailing it to the professor
    D. dictating the contents of the report to the professor over the phone

13. An office assistant is in the process of typing the forms for   13._____
recommendation for promotion for a member of the faculty who is away
for a week. She notes that two books of which he is the author are listed
without dates.
Of the following, the procedure she should BEST follow at this point
generally is to
    A. postpone doing the job until the professor returns to campus the
following week
    B. type the material omitting the books
    C. check the professor's office for copies of the books and obtain the
correct data
    D. call the professor's wife and ask her when the books were
published

14. An office has introduced work standards for all of the employees.   14._____
Of the following, it is MOST likely that use of such standards would tend
to
   A. make it more difficult to determine numbers of employees needed
   B. lead to a substantial drop in morale among all of the employees
   C. reduce the possibility of planning to meet emergencies
   D. reduce uncertainty about the costs of doing tasks

15. Of the following clerical errors, the one which probably is LEAST   15._____
important is
   A. adding 543 instead of 548 to a bookkeeping account
   B. putting the wrong code on a data processing card
   C. recording a transaction on the record of Henry Smith instead of on
the record of Harry Smith
   D. writing John Murpfy instead of John Murphy when addressing an
envelope

16. Of the following errors, the one which probably is MOST important is   16._____
   A. writing "they're" instead of "their" in an office memo
   B. misplacing a decimal point on a sales invoice
   C. forgetting to write the date on a note for a supervisor
   D. sending an e-mail to a misspelled e-mail address

17. The chairman of an academic department tells an office assistant that a   17._____
meeting of the faculty is to be held four weeks from the current date.
Of the following responsibilities, the office assistant is MOST frequently
held responsible for
   A. planning the agenda of the meeting
   B. presiding over the conduct of the meeting
   C. reserving the meeting room and notifying the members
   D. initiating all formal resolutions

18. Of the following, a centralized filing system is LEAST suitable for filing   18._____
   A. material which is confidential in nature
   B. routine correspondence
   C. periodic reports of the divisions of the department
   D. material used by several divisions of the department

19. A misplaced record is a lost record.   19._____
Of the following, the MOST valid implication of this statement in regard to
office work is that
   A. all records in an office should be filed in strict alphabetical order
   B. accuracy in filing is essential
   C. only one method of filing should be used throughout the office
   D. files should be locked when not in use

20. When typing names or titles on a roll of folder labels, the one of the
   following which is MOST important to do is to type the caption

   20._____

   A. as it appears on the papers to be placed in the folder
   B. in capital letters
   C. in exact indexing or filing order
   D. so that it appears near the bottom of the folder tab when the label
       is attached

21. A professor at a Boston university asks an office assistant to place a call
   to a fellow professor in San Francisco. The MOST appropriate local time
   for the assistant to place the call to the professor in California, given the
   time difference, would be

   21._____

   A. 8:30 a.m.   B. 10:00 a.m.   C. 11:30 a.m.   D. 1:30 p.m.

22. When typing the rough draft of a report, the computer application you
   would use is

   22._____

   A. Excel   B. Word
   C. PowerPoint   D. Internet Explorer

23. Which of the following is the BEST and most appropriate way to
   proofread and edit a report before submitting it to a supervisor for review?

   23._____

   A. Scan the report with the program's spell check feature
   B. Proof the report yourself, then ask another office assistant to read
       the report over as well until it is finished
   C. Give the report to another office assistant who is more skilled at
       proofreading
   D. Use the spell checker, then scan the report yourself as many
       times as needed in order to pick up any additional errors

24. The one of the following situations in which it would be MOST justifiable
   for an office to use standard or form paragraphs in its business letters is
   when

   24._____

   A. a large number of similar letters is to be sent
   B. the letters are to be uniform in length and appearance
   C. it is desired to reduce typing errors in correspondence
   D. the office is to carry on a lengthy correspondence with an
       individual

25. Of the following, the MOST important factor in determining whether or not
   an office filing system is effective is that the

   25._____

   A. information in the files is legible
   B. records in the files are used frequently
   C. information in the files is accurate
   D. records in the files can be located readily

KEY (CORRECT ANSWERS)

1. B	11. B	21. D
2. D	12. C	22. B
3. C	13. C	23. D
4. B	14. D	24. A
5. A	15. D	25. D
6. D	16. B	
7. A	17. C	
8. D	18. A	
9. C	19. B	
10. D	20. C	

TEST 2

DIRECTIONS: Each question or incomplete statement is followed by several suggested answers or completions. Select the one that BEST answers the question or completes the statement. *PRINT THE LETTER OF THE CORRECT ANSWER IN THE SPACE AT THE RIGHT.*

1. For the office assistant whose duties include frequent recording and transcription of minutes of formal meetings, the one of the following reference works generally considered to be MOST useful is
   A. *Robert's Rules of Order*
   B. *Bartlett's Familiar Quotations*
   C. *World Almanac and Book of Facts*
   D. *Conway's Reference*

1._____

2. Of the following statements about the numeric system of filing, the one which is CORRECT is that it
   A. is the least accurate of all methods of filing
   B. eliminates the need for cross-referencing
   C. allows for very limited expansion
   D. requires a separate index

2._____

3. When more than one name or subject is involved in a piece of correspondence to be filed, the office assistant should GENERALLY
   A. prepare a cross-reference sheet
   B. establish a geographical filing system
   C. prepare out-guides
   D. establish a separate index card file for noting such correspondence

3._____

4. A tickler file is MOST generally used for
   A. identification of material contained in a numeric file
   B. maintenance of a current listing of telephone numbers
   C. follow-up of matters requiring future attention
   D. control of records borrowed or otherwise removed from the files

4._____

5. In filing, the name Ms. *Ann Catalana-Moss* should GENERALLY be indexed as
   A. Moss, Catalana, Ann (Ms.)
   B. Catalana-Moss, Ann (Ms.)
   C. Ann Catalana-Moss (Ms.)
   D. Moss-Catalana, Ann (Ms.)

5._____

6. An office assistant has a set of four cards, each of which contains one of   6._____
the following names.
   In alphabetic filing, the FIRST of the cards to be filed is
   A. Ms. Alma John
   B. Mrs. John (Patricia) Edwards
   C. John-Edward School Supplies, Inc.
   D. John H. Edwards

7. Generally, of the following, the name to be filed FIRST in an alphabetical   7._____
filing system is
   A. Diane Maestro   B. Diana McElroy
   C. James Mackell   D. James McKell

8. After checking several times, you are unable to locate a student record in   8._____
its proper file drawer. The file drawer in question is used constantly by
many members of the staff.
   In this situation, the NEXT step you should take in locating the missing
record is to
   A. ask another worker to look through the file drawer
   B. determine if there is another copy of the record filed in a different
      place
   C. find out if the record has been removed by another staff member
   D. wait a day or two and see if the record turns up

9. It is MOST important that an enclosure which is to be mailed with a letter   9._____
should be put in an envelope so that
   A. any printing on the enclosure will not be visible through the
      address side of the envelope
   B. it is obvious that there is an enclosure inside the envelope
   C. the enclosure takes up less space than the letter
   D. the person who opens the envelope will pull out both the letter and
      the enclosure

10. Suppose that one of the student aides with whom you work suggests a   10._____
change in the filing procedure. He is sure the change will result in
increased rates of filing among the other employees.
   The one of the following which you should do FIRST is to
   A. ask him to demonstrate his method in order to determine if he files
      more quickly than the other employees
   B. ask your supervisor if you may make a change in the filing
      procedure
   C. ignore the aide's suggestion since he is not a filing expert
   D. tell him to show his method to the other employees and to
      encourage them to use it

11. It is generally advisable to leave at least six inches of working space in a   11._____
file drawer. This procedure is MOST useful in
    A. decreasing the number of filing errors
    B. facilitating the sorting of documents and folders
    C. maintaining a regular program of removing inactive records
    D. preventing folders and papers from being torn

12. Assume that a dictator is briefly interrupted because of a telephone call or   12._____
other similar matter (no more than three minutes).
Of the following tasks, the person taking the dictation should NORMALLY
use the time to
    A. re-read notes already recorded
    B. tidy the dictator's desk
    C. check the accuracy of the dictator's desk files
    D. return to her own desk to type the dictated material

13. When typing a preliminary draft of a report, the one of the following which   13._____
you should generally NOT do is
    A. erase typing errors and deletions rather than cross them out
    B. leave plenty of room at the top, bottom and sides of each page
    C. make only the number of copies that you are asked to make
    D. type double or triple space

14. The BEST way for a receptionist to deal with a situation in which she   14._____
must leave her desk for a long time is to
    A. ask someone to take her place while she is away
    B. leave a note or sign on her desk which indicates the time she will
        return
    C. take a chance that no one will arrive while she is gone and leave
        her desk unattended
    D. tell a coworker to ask any visitors that arrive to wait until she
        returns

15. Suppose that two individuals come up to your desk at the same time.   15._____
One of them asks you for the location of the nearest public phone. After
you answer the question, you turn to the second person who asks you the
same question.
The one of the following actions that would be BEST for you to take in this
situation is to
    A. ignore the second person since he obviously overheard your first
        answer
    B. point out that you just answered the same question and quickly
        repeat the information
    C. politely repeat the information to the second individual
    D. tell the second person to follow the first to the public telephone

16. Which of the following names should be filed FIRST in an alphabetical filing system?
    A. Anthony Aarvedsen   B. William Aaron
    C. Denise Aron   D. A.J. Arrington

16._____

17. New material added to a file folder should USUALLY be inserted
    A. in the order of importance (the most important in front)
    B. in the order of importance (the most important in back)
    C. chronologically (most recent in front)
    D. chronologically (most recent in back)

17._____

18. An individual is looking for a name in the White Pages of a telephone directory.
    Which of the following BEST describes the system of filing found there?
    A. alphabetic   B. sequential
    C. locator   D. index

18._____

19. The MAIN purpose of a tickler file is to
    A. help prevent overlooking matters that require future attention
    B. check on adequacy of past performance
    C. pinpoint responsibility for recurring daily tasks
    D. reduce the volume of material kept in general files

19._____

20. Which of the following BEST describes the process of *reconciling* a bank statement?
    A. Analyzing the nature of the expenditures made by the office during the preceding month
    B. Comparing the statement of the bank with the banking records maintained in the office
    C. Determining the liquidity position by reading the bank statement carefully
    D. Checking the service charges noted on the bank statement

20._____

21. From the viewpoint of preserving agency or institutional funds, the LEAST acceptable method for making a payment is a check made out to
    A. cash   B. a company
    C. an individual   D. a partnership

21._____

22. Listed below are four of the steps in the process of preparing correspondence for filing.
    If they were to be put in logical sequence, the SECOND step would be
    A. preparing cross-reference sheets or cards
    B. coding the correspondence using a classification system
    C. sorting the correspondence in the order to be filed
    D. checking for follow-up action required and preparing a follow-up slip

22._____

23. The process of *justifying* typed copy involves laying out the copy so that   23._____
    A. each paragraph appears to be approximately the same size
    B. no long words are broken up at the end of a line
    C. the right and left hand margins are even
    D. there is enough room to enter proofreading marks at the end of each line

24. The MOST important reason for a person in charge of a petty cash fund   24._____
    to obtain receipts for payments is that this practice would tend to
    A. decrease robberies by delivery personnel
    B. eliminate the need to keep a record of petty cash expenditures
    C. prove that the fund has been used properly
    D. provide a record of the need for cash in the daily operations of the office

25. You should GENERALLY replenish a petty cash fund   25._____
    A. at regularly established intervals
    B. each time you withdraw a sum
    C. when the amount of cash gets below a certain specified amount
    D. when the fund is completely empty

KEY (CORRECT ANSWERS)

1. A	11. D	21. A
2. D	12. A	22. A
3. A	13. A	23. C
4. C	14. A	24. C
5. B	15. C	25. C
6. D	16. B	
7. C	17. C	
8. C	18. A	
9. D	19. A	
10. A	20. B	

EXAMINATION SECTION
TEST 1

DIRECTIONS: Each question or incomplete statement is followed by several suggested answers or completions. Select the one that BEST answers the question or completes the statement. *PRINT THE LETTER OF THE CORRECT ANSWER IN THE SPACE AT THE RIGHT.*

1. A coworker has e-mailed a file containing a spreadsheet for your review. Which of the following programs will open the file?   1._____

    A. Adobe Reader
    B. Microsoft Excel
    C. Microsoft PowerPoint
    D. Adobe Illustrator

2. A report needs to be forwarded immediately to a supervisor in another office. Which of the following is the LEAST effective way of giving the supervisor the report?   2._____

    A. scanning the report and e-mailing the file
    B. faxing it to the supervisor's office
    C. uploading it to the office network and informing the supervisor
    D. waiting for the supervisor to come to your office and giving it to him/her then

3. Suppose your supervisor is on the telephone in his office and an applicant arrives for a scheduled interview with him.   3._____
    Of the following, the BEST procedure to follow ordinarily is to

    A. informally chat with the applicant in your office until your supervisor has finished his phone conversation
    B. escort him directly into your supervisor's office and have him wait for him there
    C. inform your supervisor of the applicant's arrival and try to make the applicant feel comfortable while waiting
    D. have him hang up his coat and tell him to go directly in to see your supervisor

Questions 4-9.

DIRECTIONS: Questions 4 through 9 each consist of a sentence which may or may not be an example of good English usage. Consider grammar, punctuation, spelling, capitalization, awkwardness, etc. Examine each sentence, and then choose the correct statement about it from the four choices below it. If the English usage in the sentence given is better than any of the changes suggested in options B, C, or D, choose option A. Do not choose an option that will change the meaning of the sentence.

4. The report, along with the accompanying documents, were submitted for review.   4._____

    A. This is an example of acceptable writing.
    B. The words *were submitted* should be changed to *was submitted.*
    C. The word *accompanying* should be spelled *accompaning.*
    D. The comma after the word *report* should be taken out.

5. If others must use your files, be certain that they understand how the system works, but   5._____
   insist that you do all the filing and refiling.

   A. This is an example of acceptable writing.
   B. There should be a period after the word *works*, and the word *but* should start a new
      sentence.
   C. The words *filing* and *refiling* should be spelled *fileing* and *refileing*.
   D. There should be a comma after the word *but*.

6. The appeal was not considered because of its late arrival.   6._____

   A. This is an example of acceptable writing.
   B. The word *its* should be changed to *it's*.
   C. The word *its* should be changed to *the*.
   D. The words *late arrival* should be changed to *arrival late*.

7. The letter must be read carefuly to determine under which subject it should be filed.   7._____

   A. This is an example of acceptable writing.
   B. The word *under* should be changed to *at*.
   C. The word *determine* should be spelled *determin*.
   D. The word *carefuly* should be spelled *carefully*.

8. He showed potential as an office manager, but he lacked skill in delegating work.   8._____

   A. This is an example of acceptable writing.
   B. The word *delegating* should be spelled *delagating*.
   C. The word *potential* should be spelled *potencial*.
   D. The words *lie lacked* should be changed to *was lacking*.

9. His supervisor told him that it would be all right to receive personal mail at the office.   9._____

   A. This is an example of acceptable writing.
   B. The words *all right* should be changed to *alright*.
   C. The word *personal* should be spelled *personel*.
   D. The word *mail* should be changed to *letters*.

Questions 10-13.

DIRECTIONS: Questions 10 through 13 are to be answered SOLELY on the basis of the information given in the following passage.

Typed pages can reflect the simplicity of modern art in a machine age. Lightness and evenness can be achieved by proper layout and balance of typed lines and white space. Instead of solid, cramped masses of uneven, crowded typing, there should be a pleasing balance up and down as well as horizontal.

To have real balance, your page must have a center. The eyes see the center of the sheet slightly above the real center. This is the way both you and the reader see it. Try imagining a line down the center of the page that divides the paper in equal halves. On either side of your paper, white space and blocks of typing need to be similar in size and shape. Although left and right margins should be equal, top and bottom margins need not be as exact. It looks better to hold a bottom border wider than a top margin, so that your typing rests upon a cushion of white space. To add interest to the appearance of the page, try making one paragraph between one-half and two-thirds the size of an adjacent paragraph.

Thus, by taking full advantage of your typewriter, the pages that you type will not only be accurate but will also be attractive.

10. It can be inferred from the passage that the BASIC importance of proper balancing on a typed page is that proper balancing

    10.____

    A. makes a typed page a work of modern art
    B. provides exercise in proper positioning of a typewriter
    C. increases the amount of typed copy on the paper
    D. draws greater attention and interest to the page

11. A reader will tend to see the center of a typed page

    11.____

    A. somewhat higher than the true center
    B. somewhat lower than the true center
    C. on either side of the true center
    D. about two-thirds of an inch above the true center

12. Which of the following suggestions is NOT given by the passage?

    12.____

    A. Bottom margins may be wider than top borders.
    B. Keep all paragraphs approximately the same size.
    C. Divide your page with an imaginary line down the middle.
    D. Side margins should be equalized.

13. Of the following, the BEST title for this passage is:

    13.____

    A. INCREASING THE ACCURACY OF THE TYPED PAGE
    B. DETERMINATION OF MARGINS FOR TYPED COPY
    C. LAYOUT AND BALANCE OF THE TYPED PAGE
    D. HOW TO TAKE FULL ADVANTAGE OF THE TYPEWRITER

14. In order to type addresses on a large number of envelopes MOST efficiently, you should

    14.____

    A. insert another envelope into the typewriter before removing each typed envelope
    B. take each typed envelope out of the machine before starting the next envelope
    C. insert several envelopes into the machine at one time, keeping all top and bottom edges even
    D. insert several envelopes into the machine at one time, keeping the top edge of each envelope two inches below the top edge of the one beneath it

15. A senior typist has completed copying a statistical report from a rough draft.
Of the following, the BEST way to be sure that her typing is correct is for the typist to

    15.____

    A. fold the rough draft, line it up with the typed copy, compare one-half of the columns with the original, and have a co-worker compare the other half
    B. check each line of the report as it is typed and then have a co-worker check each line again after the entire report is finished

C. have a co-worker add each column and check the totals on the typed copy with the totals on the original

D. have a co-worker read aloud from the rough draft while the typist checks the typed copy and then have the typist read while the co-worker checks

16. In order to center a heading when typing a report, you should   16._____

A. measure your typing paper with a ruler and begin the heading one-third of the way in from the left margin

B. begin the heading at the point on the typewriter scale which is 50 minus the number of letters in the heading

C. multiply the number of characters in the heading by two and begin the heading that number of spaces in from the left margin

D. begin the heading at the point on the scale which is equal to the center point of your paper minus one-half the number of characters and spaces in the heading

17. Which of the following recommendations concerning the use of copy paper for making   17._____
typewritten copies should NOT be followed?

A. Copy papers should be checked for wrinkles before being used.

B. Legal-size copy paper may be folded if it is too large to fit into a convenient drawer space.

C. When several sheets of paper are being used, they should be fastened with a paper clip at the top after insertion in the typewriter.

D. For making many copies, paper of the same weight and brightness should be used.

18. Assume that a new typist, Norma Garcia, has been assigned to work under your supervi-   18._____
sion and is reporting to work for the first time. You formally introduce Norma to her co-
workers and suggest that a few of the other typists explain the office procedures and typing formats to her. The practice of instructing Norma in her duties in this manner is

A. *good* because she will be made to feel at home

B. *good* because she will learn more about routine office tasks from co-workers than from you

C. *poor* because her co-workers will resent the extra work

D. *poor* because you will not have enough control over her training

19. Suppose that Jean Brown, a typist, is typing a letter following the same format that she   19._____
has always used. However, she notices that the other two typists in her office are also
typing letters, but are using a different format. Jean is concerned that she might not have
been informed of a change in format.
Of the following, the FIRST action that Jean should take is to

A. seek advice from her supervisor as to which format to use

B. ask the other typists whether she should use a new format for typing letters

C. disregard the format that the other typists are using and continue to type in the format she had been using

D. use the format that the other typists are using, assuming that it is a newly accepted method

20. Suppose that the new office to which you have been assigned has put up Christmas dec-   20. ____
orations, and a Christmas party is being planned by the city agency in which you work.
However, nothing has been said about Christmas gifts.
It would be CORRECT for you to assume that

    A.   you are expected to give a gift to your supervisor
    B.   your supervisor will give you a gift
    C.   you are expected to give gifts only to your subordinates
    D.   you will neither receive gifts nor will you be expected to give any

---

KEY (CORRECT ANSWERS)

1.	B	11.	A
2.	D	12.	B
3.	C	13.	C
4.	B	14.	A
5.	A	15.	D
6.	A	16.	D
7.	D	17.	B
8.	A	18.	D
9.	A	19.	A
10.	D	20.	D

TEST 2

DIRECTIONS: Each question or incomplete statement is followed by several suggested answers or completions. Select the one that BEST answers the question or completes the statement. *PRINT THE LETTER OF THE CORRECT ANSWER IN THE SPACE AT THE RIGHT.*

1. The supervisor you assist is under great pressure to meet certain target dates. He has scheduled an emergency meeting to take place in a few days, and he asks you to send out notices immediately. As you begin to prepare the notices, however, you realize he has scheduled the meeting for a Saturday, which is not a working day. Also, you sense that your supervisor is not in a good mood.
Which of the following is the MOST effective method of handling this situation?

    A. Change the meeting date to the first working day after that Saturday and send out the notices.
    B. Change the meeting date to a working day on which his calendar is clear and send out the notices.
    C. Point out to your supervisor that the date is a Saturday.
    D. Send out the notices as they are since you have received specific instructions.

1.____

Questions 2-7.

DIRECTIONS: Questions 2 through 7 each consist of a sentence which may or may not be an example of good English usage. Consider grammar, punctuation, spelling, capitalization, awkwardness, etc. Examine each sentence, and then choose the correct statement about it from the four choices below it. If the English usage in the sentence given is better than any of the changes suggested in options B, C, or D, choose option A. Do not choose an option that will change the meaning of the sentence.

2. The typist used an extention cord in order to connect her typewriter to the outlet nearest to her desk.

    A. This is an example of acceptable writing.
    B. A period should be placed after the word *cord,* and the word *in* should have a capital I.
    C. A comma should be placed after the word *typewriter.*
    D. The word *extention* should be spelled *extension.*

2.____

3. He would have went to the conference if he had received an invitation.

    A. This is an example of acceptable writing.
    B. The word *went* should be replaced by the word *gone.*
    C. The word *had* should be replaced by *would have.*
    D. The word *conference* should be spelled *conferance.*

3.____

4. In order to make the report neater, he spent many hours rewriting it.

    A. This is an example of acceptable writing.
    B. The word *more* should be inserted before the word *neater.*
    C. There should be a colon after the word *neater.*
    D. The word *spent* should be changed to *have spent.*

4.____

5. His supervisor told him that he should of read the memorandum more carefully.   5.____

    A. This is an example of acceptable writing.
    B. The word *memorandum* should be spelled *memorandom*.
    C. The word *of* should be replaced by the word *have*.
    D. The word *carefully* should be replaced by the word *careful*.

6. It was decided that two separate reports should be written.   6.____

    A. This is an example of acceptable writing.
    B. A comma should be inserted after the word *decided*.
    C. The word *be* should be replaced by the word *been*.
    D. A colon should be inserted after the word *that*.

7. She don't seem to understand that the work must be done as soon as possible.   7.____

    A. This is an example of acceptable writing.
    B. The word *doesn't* should replace the word *don't*.
    C. The word *why* should replace the word *that*.
    D. The word *as* before the word *soon* should be eliminated.

Questions 8-11.

DIRECTIONS: Questions 8 through 11 are to be answered SOLELY on the basis of the following passage.

There is nothing that will take the place of good sense on the part of the stenographer. You may be perfect in transcribing exactly what the dictator says and your speed may be adequate; but without an understanding of the dictator's intent as well as his words, you are likely to be a mediocre secretary.

A serious error that is made when taking dictation is putting down something that does not make sense. Most people who dictate material would rather be asked to repeat and explain than to receive transcribed material which has errors due to inattention or doubt. Many dictators request that their grammar be corrected by their secretaries; but unless specifically asked to do so, secretaries should not do it without first checking with the dictator. Secretaries should be aware that, in some cases, dictators may use incorrect grammar or slang expressions to create a particular effect.

Some people dictate commas, periods, and paragraphs, while others expect the stenographer to know when, where, and how to punctuate. A well-trained secretary should be able to indicate the proper punctuation by listening to the pauses and tones of the dictator's voice.

A stenographer who has taken dictation from the same person for a period of time should be able to understand him under most conditions. By increasing her tact, alertness, and efficiency, a secretary can become more competent.

8. According to the passage, which of the following statements concerning the dictation of punctuation is CORRECT?   8.____
A

    A. dictator may use incorrect punctuation to create a desired style

B. dictator should indicate all punctuation
C. stenographer should know how to punctuate based on the pauses and tones of the dictator
D. stenographer should not type any punctuation if it has not been dictated to her

9. According to the passage, how should secretaries handle grammatical errors in a dictation?
Secretaries should

9._____

A. *not correct* grammatical errors unless the dictator is aware that this is being done
B. *correct* grammatical errors by having the dictator repeat the line with proper pauses
C. *correct* grammatical errors if they have checked the correctness in a grammar book
D. *correct* grammatical errors based on their own good sense

10. If a stenographer is confused about the method of spacing and indenting of a report which has just been dictated to her, she GENERALLY should

10._____

A. do the best she can
B. ask the dictator to explain what she should do
C. try to improve her ability to understand dictated material
D. accept the fact that her stenographic ability is not adequate

11. In the last line of the first paragraph, the word *mediocre* means MOST NEARLY

11._____

A. superior
C. respected
B. disregarded
D. second-rate

12. Assume that is is your responsibility to schedule meetings for your supervisor, who believes in starting these meetings strictly on time. He has told you to schedule separate meetings with Mr. Smith and Ms. Jones, which will last approximately 20 minutes each. You have told Mr. Smith to arrive at 10:00 A.M. and Ms. Jones at 10:30 A.M. Your supervisor will have an hour of free time at 11:00 A.M. At 10:25 A.M., Mr. Smith arrives and states that there was a train delay, and he is sorry that he is late. Ms. Jones has not yet arrived. You do not know who Mr. Smith and Ms. Jones are or what the meetings will be about.
Of the following, the BEST course of action for you to take is to

12._____

A. send Mr. Smith in to see your supervisor; and when Ms. Jones arrives, tell her that your supervisor's first meeting will take more time than he expected
B. tell Mr. Smith that your supervisor has a meeting at 10:30 A.M. and that you will have to reschedule his meeting for another day
C. check with your supervisor to find out if he would prefer to see Mr. Smith immediately or at 11:00 A.M.
D. encourage your supervisor to meet with Mr. Smith immediately because Mr. Smith's late arrival was not intentional

13. Assume that you have been told by your boss not to let anyone disturb him for the rest of the afternoon unless absolutely necessary since he has to complete some urgent work. His supervisor, who is the bureau chief, telephones and asks to speak to him.
The BEST course of action for you to take is to

13._____

A.   ask the bureau chief if he can leave a message
B.   ask your boss if he can take the call
C.   tell the bureau chief that your boss is out
D.   tell your boss that his instructions will get you into trouble

14.   Which one of the following is the MOST advisable procedure for a stenographer to follow   14.____
when a dictator asks her to make extra copies of dictated material?

A.   Note the number of copies required at the beginning of the notes.
B.   Note the number of copies required at the end of the notes.
C.   Make a mental note of the number of copies required to be made.
D.   Make a checkmark beside the notes to serve as a reminder that extra copies are required.

15.   Suppose that, as you are taking shorthand notes, the dictator tells you that the sentence   15.____
he has just dictated is to be deleted.
Of the following, the BEST thing for you to do is to

A.   place the correction in the left-hand margin next to the deleted sentence
B.   write the word *delete* over the sentence and place the correction on a separate page for corrections
C.   erase the sentence and use that available space for the correction
D.   draw a line through the sentence and begin the correction on the next available line

16.   Assume that your supervisor, who normally dictates at a relatively slow rate, begins dic-   16.____
tating to you very rapidly. You find it very difficult to keep up at this speed. Which one of
the following is the BEST action to take in this situation?

A.   Ask your supervisor to dictate more slowly since you are having difficulty.
B.   Continue to take the dictation at the fast speed and fill in the blanks later.
C.   Interrupt your supervisor with a question about the dictation, hoping that when she begins again it will be slower.
D.   Refuse to take the dictation unless given at the speed indicated in your job description.

17.   Assume that you have been asked to put a heading on the second, third, and fourth   17.____
pages of a four-page letter to make sure they can be identified in case they are separated from the first page.
Which of the following is it LEAST important to include in such a heading?

A.   Date of the letter
B.   Initials of the typist
C.   Name of the person to whom the letter is addressed
D.   Number of the page

18.   Which one of the following is NOT generally accepted when dividing words at the end of   18.____
a line?
Dividing

A.   a hyphenated word at the hyphen
B.   a word immediately after the prefix
C.   a word immediately before the suffix
D.   proper names between syllables

19. In the preparation of a business letter which has two enclosures, the MOST generally accepted of the following procedures to follow is to type

    19.____

    A. *See Attached Items* one line below the last line of the body of the letter
    B. *See Attached Enclosures* to the left of the signature
    C. *Enclosures 2* at the left margin below the signature line
    D. nothing on the letter to indicate enclosures since it will be obvious to the reader that there are enclosures in the envelope

20. Standard rules for typing spacing have developed through usage. According to these rules, one space is left AFTER

    20.____

    A. a comma   B. every sentence
    C. a colon   D. an opening parenthesis

KEY (CORRECT ANSWERS)

1.	C	11.	D
2.	D	12.	C
3.	B	13.	B
4.	A	14.	A
5.	C	15.	D
6.	A	16.	A
7.	B	17.	B
8.	C	18.	D
9.	A	19.	C
10.	B	20.	A

EXAMINATION SECTION
TEST 1

DIRECTIONS: Each question or incomplete statement is followed by several suggested answers or completions. Select the one that BEST answers the question or completes the statement. *PRINT THE LETTER OF THE CORRECT ANSWER IN THE SPACE AT THE RIGHT.*

Questions 1-25

Each sentence in questions 1-25 includes four words with letters over them. One of these words has been typed incorrectly. Indicate the misspelled word by printing the letter in the space at the right.

1.   A   B   1.____

                    A   B
If the administrator attempts to withold information,
                  C
there is a good likelihood that there will be serious
        D
repercussions.

2.   2.____

               A   B   C
He condescended to apologize, but we felt that a beligerent
                                      D
person should not occupy an influential position.

3.   3.____

                    A   B   C
Despite the sporadic delinquent payments of his indebted-
                              D
ness, Mr. Johnson has been an exemplery customer.

4.   4.____

                      A   B
He was appreciative of the support he consistantly
            C   D
acquired, but he felt that he had waited an inordinate
length of time for it.

5.   5.____

                    A   B
Undeniably they benefited from the establishment of a
            C   D
receivership, but the question or statutary limitations
remained unresolved.

6.   6.____

                  A

Mr. Smith profered his hand as an indication that he

                    B   C

considered it a viable contract, but Mr. Nelson alluded

                      D

to the fact that his colleagues had not been consulted.

7.   7.____

                        A   B

The treatments were beneficial according to the optomo-

                  C   D

trists, and the consensus was that minimal improvement

could be expected.

8.   8.____

                A

Her frivalous manner was unbecoming because the air of

        B   C   D

solemnity at the cemetery was pervasive.

9.   9.____

                  A

The clandestine meetings were designed to make the two

        B   C

adversaries more amicible, but they served only to

                  D

intensify their emnity.

10.   10.____

                      A

Do you think that his innovative ideas and financial

        B   C   D

acumen will help stabalize the fluctuations of the stock

market?

11.   11.____

                    A

In order to keep a perpetual inventory, you will have to

                    B   C   D

keep an uninterrupted surveillance of all the miscellaneous

stock.

12.   12.____

                    A

She used the art of pursuasion on the children because

                  B   C   D

she found that caustic remarks had no perceptible effect

on their behavior.

13.   13._____

                     A   B
His sacreligious outbursts offended his constituents , and
                        C   D
he was summarily removed from office by the City Council.

14.   14._____

                     A   B
They exhorted the contestants to greater efforts, but the
                 C
exhorbitant costs in terms of energy expended resulted in
                       D
a feeling of lethargy.

15.   15._____

                            A   B
Since he was knowledgable about illicit drugs, he was
                      C   D
served with a subpoena to appear for the prosecution.

16.   16._____

                       A   B
In spite of his lucid statements, they denigrated his
                                 C   D
report and decided it should be succintly paraphrased.

17.   17._____

                                 A   B
The discussion was not germane to the contraversy, but
                   C   D
the indicted man's insistence on further talk was allowed.

18.   18._____

                   A   B
The legislators were enervated by the distances they had
          C   D
traveled during the election year to fulfil their speaking
engagements.

19.   19._____

                   A   B   C
The plaintiffs' attornies charged the defendant in the
                         D
case with felonious assault.

20.   20._____

                   A   B

It is symptomatic of the times that we try to placate

                                           C

all, but a proposal for new forms of disciplinery action

                  D

was promulgated by the staff.

21.   21._____

                  A

A worrysome situation has developed as a result of the

               B   C

assessment that absenteeism is increasing despite our

               D

conscientious efforts.

22.   22._____

                   A   B

I concurred with the credit manager that it was practi-

                                 C

cable to charge purchases on a biennial basis, and the

                          D

company agreed to adhear to this policy.

23.   23._____

                             A   B   C

The pastor was chagrined and embarassed by the irreverent

                                D

conduct of one of his parishioners.

24.   24._____

                   A   B   C

His inate seriousness was belied by his flippant

D

demeanor.

25.   25._____

                   A   B   C

It was exceedingly regrettable that the excessive number

                  D

of challanges in the court delayed the start of the

trial.

Questions 26-45.

In each of the following sentences, numbered 26-45, <u>there may be an error.</u> Indicate the appropriate correction by printing the corresponding letter in the space at the right. If the sentence is correct as is, indicate this by printing the corresponding letter in the space at the right. <u>Unnecessary changes will be considered incorrect.</u>

26. In that building there seemed to be representatives of Teachers College, the Veterans Bureau, and the Businessmen's Association.   26.____

   A. Teacher's College   B. Veteran's Bureau
   C. Businessmens Association   D. correct as is

27. In his travels, he visited St. Paul, San Francisco, Springfield, Ohio, and Washington, D.C..   27.____

   A. Ohio and   B. Saint Paul
   C. Washington, D.C.   D. correct as is

28. As a result of their purchasing a controlling interest in the syndicate, it was well-known that the Bureau of Labor Statistics' calculations would be unimportant.   28.____

   A. of them purchasing   B. well known
   C. Statistics   D. correct as is

29. Walter Scott, Jr.'s, attempt to emulate his father's success was doomed to failure.   29.____

   A. Junior's,   B. Scott's, Jr.,
   C. Scott, Jr.'s attempt   D. correct as is

30. About B.C. 250 the Romans invaded Great Britain, and remains of their highly developed civilization can still be seen.   30.____

   A. 250 B.C.   B. Britain and
   C. highly-developed   D. correct as is

31. The two boss's sons visited the children's department.   31.____

   A. bosses   B. bosses'
   C. childrens'   D. correct as is

32. Miss Amex not only approved the report, but also decided that it needed no revision.   32.____

   A. report; but   B. report but
   C. report. But   D. correct as is

33. Here's brain food in a jiffy--economical too!   33.____

   A. economical too!   B. 'brain food'
   C. jiffy-economical   D. correct as is

34. She said, "He likes the "Gatsby Look" very much."   34.____

   A. said "He   B. "he
   C. 'Gatsby Look'   D. correct as is

35. We anticipate that we will be able to visit them briefly in Los Angeles on Wednesday after a 5-day visit.

    A. Wednes-   B. 5-day
    C. briefly   D. correct as is

35.____

36. She passed all her tests, and, she now has a good position.

    A. tests, and she   B. past
    C. tests;   D. correct as is

36.____

37. The billing clerk said, "I will send the bill today"; however, that was a week ago, and it hasn't arrived yet!

    A. today;"   B. today,"
    C. ago and   D. correct as is

37.____

38. "She types at more-than-average speed," Miss Smith said, "but I feel that it is a result of marvelous concentration and self control on her part."

    A. more than average   B. "But
    C. self-control   D. correct as is

38.____

39. The state of Alaska, the largest state in the union, is also the northernmost state.

    A. Union   B. Northernmost State
    C. State of Alaska   D. correct as is

39.____

40. The memoirs of Ex-President Nixon, will sell more copies than Six Crises, the book he wrote in the 60's.

    A. Six Crises   B. ex-President
    C. 60s   D. correct as is

40.____

41. He spoke on his favorite topic, "Why We Will Win." (How could I stop him?)

    A. Win".   B. him?).
    C. him)?   D. correct as is

41.____

42. "All any insurance policy is, is a contract for services," said my insurance agent, Mr. Newton.

    A. Insurance Policy   B. Insurance Agent
    C. policy is is a   D. correct as is

42.____

43. Inasmuch as the price list has not been up dated, we should send it to the printer.

    A. In as much   B. updated
    C. pricelist   D. correct as is

43.____

44. We feel that "Our know-how" is responsible for the improvement in technical developments.

    A. "our   B. know how
    C. that,   D. correct as is

44.____

45. Did Cortez conquer the Incas? the Aztecs? the South American Indians?

    A. Incas, the Aztecs, the South American Indians?
    B. Incas; the Aztecs; the South American Indians?
    C. south American Indians?
    D. correct as is

45.____

Questions 46-70.

In the article which follows, certain words or groups of words are underlined and numbered. The underlined word or group of words may be incorrect because they present an error in grammer, usage, sentence structure, capitalization, diction, or punctuation. For each numbered word or group of words, there is an identically numbered question consisting of four choices based only on the underlined portion. For each question numbered 46-70, indicate the best choice by printing the corresponding letter in the space at the right. Unnecessary changes will be considered incorrect.

TIGERS VIE FOR CITY CHAMPIONSHIP

In their second year of varsity football, the North Side Tigers have gained a shot at the city championship. Last Saturday in the play-offs, the Tigers defeated the Western High School
46
Cowboys, thus eliminated that team from contention. Most of the credit for the team's improvement must go to Joe Harris, the
47
coach. To play as well as they do now, the coach must have given the team superior instruction. There is no doubt that, if a
48
coach is effective, his influence is over many young minds.

With this major victory behind them, the Tigers can now look
49
forward to meet the defending champions, the Revere Minutemen, in the finals.
50
The win over the Cowboys was due to North Side's supremacy in the air. The Tigers' players have the advantage of strength
51
and of being speedy. Our sterling quarterback, Butch Carter, a
52
master of the long pass, used these kind of passes to bedevil the
53
boys from Western. As a matter of fact, if the Tigers would have used the passing offense earlier in the game, the score would have been more one sided. Butch, by the way, our all-around senior student, has already been tapped for bigger things. Having the
54
highest marks in his class, Barton College has offered him a scholarship.

The team's defense is another story. During the last few
55
weeks, neither the linebackers nor the safety man have shown sufficient ability to contain their opponents' running game. In
56
the city final, the defensive unit's failing to complete it's assignments may lead to disaster. However, the coach said that
57
this unit not only has been cooperative, but also the coach praised their eagerness to learn. He also said that this team
58

has not and never will give up. This kind of spirit is contag-
                59
ious, therefore I predict that the Tigers will win because I have
                60
affection and full confidence in the team.
        One of the happy surprises this season is Peter Yisko, our
                61
punter. Peter is in the United States for only two years. When
he was in grammar school in the old country, it was not necessary
                62
for him to have studied hard. Now, he depends on the football
                                63
team to help him with his English. Everybody but the team mascot
and I have been pressed into service. Peter was ineligible last
                64
year when he learned that he would only obtain half of the credits
he had completed in Europe. Nevertheless, he attended occasional
practice sessions, but he soon found out that, if one wants to be
                65
a successful player, you must realize that regular practice is
required. In fact, if a team is to be successful, it is necessary
                66
that everyone be present for all practice sessions. "The life of
                                67
a football player," says Peter, "is better than a scholar."
Facing the Minutemen, the Tigers will meet their most
                                68
formidable opposition yet. This team is not only gaining a bad
reputation but also indulging in illegal practices on the field.
                69
They can't hardly object to us being technical about penalties
under these circumstances. As far as the Minutemen are concerned,
                70
a victory will taste sweet like a victory should.

46.   A.   , that eliminated that team
      B.   and they were eliminated
      C.   and eliminated them
      D.   correct as is

46._____

47.   A.   To make them play as well as they do
      B.   Having played so well
      C.   After they played so well
      D.   correct as is

47._____

48.   A.   if coaches are effective; they have influence over
      B.   to be effective, a coach influences
      C.   if a coach is effective, he influences
      D.   correct as is

48._____

49.   49._____

    A. to meet with   B. to meeting
    C. to a meeting of   D. correct as is

50.   50._____

    A. because of   B. on account *of*
    C. motivated by   D. correct as is

51.   51._____

    A. operating swiftly   B. speed
    C. running speedily   D. correct as is

52.   52._____

    A. these kinds of pass   B. this kind of passes
    C. this kind of pass   D. correct as is

53.   53._____

    A. would be used   B. had used
    C. were using   D. correct as is

54.   A. he was offered a scholarship by Barton College.   54._____
       B. Barton College offered a scholarship to him.
       C. a scholarship was offered him by Barton College.
       D. correct as is

55.   55._____

    A. had shown   B. were showing
    C. has shown   D. correct as is

56.   A. the defensive unit failing to complete its assignment   56._____
       B. the defensive unit's failing to complete its assignment
       C. the defensive unit failing to complete it's assignment
       D. correct as is

57.   A. has been not only cooperative, but also eager to learn   57._____
       B. has not only been cooperative, but also shows eagerness to learn
       C. has been not only cooperative, but also they were eager to learn
       D. correct as is

58.   A. has not given up and never will   58._____
       B. has not and never would give up
       C. has not given up and never will give up
       D. correct as is

59.   59._____

    A. .Therefore   B. : therefore
    C. --therefore   D. correct as is

60. A. full confidence and affection for   60.____
     B. affection for and full confidence in
     C. affection and full confidence concerning
     D. correct as is

61.   61.____

     A. is living   B. was living
     C. has been   D. correct as is

62.   62.____

     A. to study   B. to be studying
     C. to have been studying   D. correct as is

63. A. but the team mascot and me has   63.____
     B. but the team mascot and myself has
     C. but the team mascot and me have
     D. correct as is

64. A. only learned that he would obtain hall   64.____
     B. learned that he would obtain only half
     C. learned that he only would obtain half
     D. correct as is

65.   65.____

     A. a person   B. everyone
     C. one   D. correct as is

66.   66.____

     A. is   B. will be
     C. shall be   D. correct as is

67.   67.____

     A. to be a scholar   B. being a scholar
     C. that of a scholar   D. correct as is

68. A. not only is gaining a bad reputation   68.____
     B. is gaining not only a bad reputation
     C. is not gaining only a bad reputation
     D. correct as is

69. A. can hardly object to us being   69.____
     B. can hardly object to our being
     C. can't hardly object to our being
     D. correct as is

70. A. victory will taste sweet like it should.   70.____
     B. victory will taste sweetly as it should taste.
     C. victory will taste sweet as a victory should.
     D. correct as is

KEY (CORRECT ANSWERS

1. B	16. C	31. B	46. C	61. C
2. C	17. B	32. B	47. A	62. A
3. D	18. D	33. D	48. C	63. A
4. B	19. B	34. C	49. B	64. B
5. D	20. C	35. B	50. A	65. C
6. A	21. A	36. A	51. B	66. D
7. B	22. D	37. D	52. C	67. C
8. A	23. B	38. D	53. B	68. D
9. C	24. A	39. A	54. D	69. A
10. C	25. D	40. B	55. C	70. C
11. D	26. D	41. D	56. B	
12. A	27. C	42. D	57. A	
13. A	28. B	43. B	58. B	
14. C	29. D	44. A	59. A	
15. A	30. A	45. D	60. B	

BASIC FUNDAMENTALS OF FILING SCIENCE

TABLE OF CONTENTS

BASIC FUNDAMENTALS OF FILING SCIENCE

I. COMMENTARY

      Filing is the systematic arrangement and storage of papers, cards, forms, catalogues, etc., so that they may be found easily and quickly. The importance of an efficient filing system cannot be emphasized too strongly. The filed materials form records which may be needed quickly to settle questions that may cause embarrassing situations if such evidence is not available. In addition to keeping papers in order so that they are readily available, the filing system must also be designed to keep papers in good condition. A filing system must be planned so that papers may be filed easily, withdrawn easily, and as quickly returned to their proper place. The cost of a filing system is also an important factor.

      The need for a filing system arose when the business man began to carry on negotiations on a large scale. He could no longer be intimate with the details of his business. What was needed in the early era was a spindle or pigeon-hole desk. Filing in pigeon-hole desks is now almost completely extinct. It was an unsatisfactory practice since pigeon holes were not labeled, and the desk was an untidy mess.

II. BASIS OF FILING

      The science of filing is an exact one and entails a thorough understanding of basic facts, materials, and methods. An overview of this important information now follows.

1. <u>Types of files</u>

    (1) SHANNON FILE

      This consists of a board, at one end of which are fastened two arches which may be opened laterally.

    (2) SPINDLE FILE

      This consists of a metal or wood base to which is attached a long, pointed spike. Papers are pushed down on the spike as received. This file is useful for temporary retention of papers.

    (3) BOX FILE

      This is a heavy cardboard or metal box, opening from the side like a book.

    (4) FLAT FILE

      This consists of a series of shallow drawers or trays, arranged like drawers in a cabinet.

    (5) BELLOWS FILE

      This is a heavy cardboard container with alphabetized or compartment sections, the ends of which are closed in such a manner that they resemble an accordion.

    (6) VERTICAL FILE

      This consists of one or more drawers in which the papers are stood on edge, usually in folders, and are indexed by guides. A series of two or more drawers in one unit is the usual file cabinet.

    (7) CLIP FILE

      This file has a large clip attached to a board and is very similar to the *SHANNON FILE*.

    (8) VISIBLE FILE

      Cards are filed flat in an overlapping arrangement which leaves a part of each card visible at all times.

    (9) ROTARY FILE

The *ROTARY FILE* has a number of visible card files attached to a post around which they can be revolved. The wheel file has visible cards which rotate around a horizontal axle.

(10) TICKLER FILE

This consists of cards or folders marked with the days of the month, in which materials are filed and turned up on the appropriate day of the month.

2. Aids in filing

(1) GUIDES

Guides are heavy cardboard, pasteboard, or bristol-board sheets the same size as folders. At the top is a tab on which is marked or printed the distinguishing letter, words, or numbers indicating the material filed in a section of the drawer.

(2) SORTING TRAYS

Sorting trays are equipped with alphabetical guides to facilitate the sorting of papers preparatory to placing them in a file.

(3) CODING

Once the classification or indexing caption has been determined, it must be indicated on the letter for filing purposes.

(4) CROSS REFERENCE

Some letters or papers might easily be called for under two or more captions. For this purpose, a cross-reference card or sheet is placed in the folder or in the index.

3. Variations of filing systems

(1) VARIADEX ALPHABETIC INDEX

Provides for more effective expansion of the alphabetic system.

(2) TRIPLE-CHECK NUMERIC FILING

Entails a multiple cross-reference, as the name implies.

(3) VARIADEX FILING

Makes use of color as an aid in filing.

(4) DEWEY DECIMAL SYSTEM

The system is a numeric one used in libraries or for filing library materials in an office. This special type of filing system is used where material is grouped in finely divided categories, such as in libraries. With this method, all material to be filed is divided into ten major groups, from 000 to 900, and then subdivided into tens, units, and decimals.

4. Centralized filing

Centralized filing means keeping the files in one specific or central location. Decentralized filing means putting away papers in files of individual departments. The first step in the organization of a central filing department is to make a careful canvass of all desks in the offices. In this manner we can determine just what material needs to be filed, and what information each desk occupant requires from the central file. Only papers which may be used at some time by persons in the various offices should be placed in the central file. A paper that is to be used at some time by persons in the various offices should be placed in the central file. A paper that is to be used by one department only should never be filed in the central file.

5. Methods of filing

While there are various methods used for filing, actually there are only five basic systems: alphabetical, subject, numerical, geographic, and chronological. All other systems are derived from one of these or from a combination of two or more of them.

Since the purpose of a filing system is to store business records <u>systemically</u> so that any particular record can be found almost instantly when required, filing requires, in addition to the proper kinds of equipment and supplies, an effective method of indexing.

There are five basic systems of filing:

(1) ALPHABETIC FILING

Most filing is alphabetical. Other methods, as described below, require extensive alphabetization.

In alphabetic filing, lettered dividers or guides are arranged in alphabetic sequence. Material to be filed is placed behind the proper guide. All materials under each letter are also arranged alphabetically. Folders are used unless the file is a card index.

(2) SUBJECT FILING

This method is used when a single, complete file on a certain subject is desired. A subject file is often maintained to assemble all correspondence on a certain subject. Such files are valuable in connection with insurance claims, contract negotiations, personnel, and other investigations, special programs, and similar subjects.

(3) GEOGRAPHICAL FILE

Materials are filed according to location: states, cities, counties, or other subdivisions. Statistics and tax information are often filed in this manner.

(4) CHRONOLOGICAL FILE

Records are filed according to date. This method is used especially in "tickler" files that have guides numbered 1 to 31 for each day of the month. Each number indicates the day of the month when the filed item requires attention.

(5) NUMERICAL FILE

This method requires an alphabetic card index giving name and number. The card index is used to locate records numbered consecutively in the files according to date received or sequence in which issued, such as licenses, permits, etc.

6. <u>Indexing</u>

Determining the name or title under which an item is to be filed is known as <u>indexing</u>. For example, how would a letter from Robert E. Smith be filed? The name would be rearranged Smith,Robert E., so that the letter would be filed under the last name.

7. <u>Alphabetizing</u>

The arranging of names for filing is known as <u>alphabetizing</u>. For example, suppose you have four letters indexed under the names Johnson, Becker, Roe, and Stern. How should these letters be arranged in the files so that they may be found easily? You would arrange the four names alphabetically, thus, Becker, Johnson, Roe, and Stern.

III. RULES FOR INDEXING AND ALPHABETIZING

1. The names of persons are to be transposed. Write the surname first, then the given name, and, finally, the middle name or initial. Then arrange the various names according to the alphabetic order of letters throughout the entire name. If there is a title, consider that after the middle name or initial.

NAMES	*INDEXED AS*
Arthur L.Bright	Bright, Arthur L.
Arthur S.Bright	Bright, Arthur S.
P.E. Cole	Cole, P.E.

Dr. John C. Fox	Fox, John C. (Dr.)

2. If a surname includes the same letters of another surname, with one or more additional letters added to the end, the shorter surname is placed first regardless of the given name or the initial of the given name.

NAMES	INDEXED AS
Robert E. Brown	Brown, Robert E.
Gerald A. Browne	Browne, Gerald A.
William O. Brownell	Brownell, William O.

3. Firm names are alphabetized under the surnames. Words like the, an, a, of, and for, are not considered.

NAMES	INDEXED AS
Bank of America	Bank of America
Bank Discount Dept.	Bank Discount Dept.
The Cranford Press	Cranford Press, The
Nelson Dwyer & Co.	Dwyer, Nelson, & Co.
Sears, Roebuck & Co.	Sears, Roebuck & Co.
Montgomery Ward & Co.	Ward, Montgomery, & Co.

4. The order of filing is determined first of all by the first letter of the names to be filed. If the first letters are the same, the order is determined by the second letters, and so on. In the following pairs of names, the order is determined by the letters underlined:

Au̲sten Ha̲yes Han̲son Harv̲ey Heat̲h Gree̲n Schwart̲z
Ba̲ker He̲ath Har̲per Harw̲ood Heato̲n Gree̲n̲e Schwar̲z

5. When surnames are alike, those with initials only precede those with given names, unless the first initial comes alphabetically after the first letter of the name.

Gleason, S.   *but,*   Abbott, Mary
Gleason, S.W.   Abbott, W.B.
Gleason, Sidney

6. Hyphenated names are treated as if spelled without the hyphen.

Lloyd, Paul N.   Lloyd, Robert
Lloyd-Jones, James   Lloyd-Thomas, A.S.

7. Company names composed of single letters which are not used as abbreviations precede the other names beginning with the same letter.

B & S Garage   E Z Duplicator Co.
B X Cable Co.   Eagle Typewriter Co.
Babbitt, R.N.   Edison Company

8. The ampersand (&) and the apostrophe (') in firm names are disregarded in alphabetizing.

Nelson & Niller   M & C Amusement Corp.
Nelson, Walter J.   M C Art Assn.
Nelson's Bakery

9. Names beginning with Mac, Mc, or M' are usually placed in regular order as spelled. Some filing systems file separately names beginning with Mc.

MacDonald, R.J.   Mazza, Anthony
Macdonald, S.B.   McAdam, Wm.
Mace, Wm.   McAndrews, Jerry

10. Names beginning with St. are listed as if the name Saint were spelled in full. Numbered street names and all abbreviated names are treated as if spelled out in full.

Saginaw   Fifth Avenue Hotel   Hart Mfg. Co.
St. Louis   42nd Street Dress Shop Hart, Martin
St. Peter's Rectory Hart, Chas.   Hart, Thos.

Sandford	Hart, Charlotte	Hart, Thomas A.
Smith, Wm.	Hart, Jas.	Hart, Thos. R.
Smith, Willis	Hart, Janice	

11. Federal, state, or city departments of government should be placed alphabetically under the governmental branch controlling them.

> Illinois, State of -- Departments and Commissions
> > Banking Dept.
> > Employment Bureau
> United States Government Departments
> > Commerce
> > Defense
> > State
> > Treasury

12. Alphabetic order

Each word in a name is an indexing unit. Arrange the names in alphabetic order by comparing similar units in each name. Consider the second units only when the first units are identical. Consider the third units only when both the first and second units are identical.

13. Single surnames or initials

A surname, when used alone, precedes the same surname with a first name or initial. A surname with a first initial only precedes a surname with a complete first name. This rule is sometimes stated, "nothing comes before something."

14. Surname prefixes

A surname prefix is not a separate indexing unit, but it is considered part of the surname. These prefixes include: d', D', Da, de, De, Del, Des, Di, Du, Fitz., La, Le, Mc, Mac, 'c, O', St., Van, Van der, Von, Von der, and others. The prefixes M', Mac, and Mc are indexed and filed exactly as they are spelled.

15. Names of firms

Names of firms and institutions are indexed and filed exactly as they are written when they do not contain the complete name of an individual.

16. Names of firms containing complete individual names

When the firm or institution name includes the complete name of an individual, the units are transposed for indexing in the same way as the name of an individual.

17. Article "The"

When the article the occurs at the beginning of a name, it is placed at the end in parentheses but it is not moved. In both cases, it is not an indexing unit and is disregarded in filing.

18. Hyphenated names

Hyphenated firm names are considered as separate indexing units. Hyphenated surnames of individuals are considered as one indexing unit; this applies also to hyphenated names of individuals whose complete names are part of a firm name.

19. Abbreviations

Abbreviations are considered as though the name were written in full; however, single letters other than abbreviations are considered as separate indexing units.

20. Conjunctions, prepositions and firm endings

Conjunctions and prepositions, such as and, for, in, of, are disregarded in indexing and filing but are not omitted or their order changed when writing names on cards and folders. Firm endings, such as Ltd., Inc., Co., Son, Bros., Mfg., and Corp., are treated as a unit in indexing and filing and are considered as though spelled in full, such as Brothers and Incorporated.

21. One or two words

    Names that may be spelled either as one or two words are indexed and filed as one word.

22. Compound geographic names

    Compound geographic names are considered as separate indexing and filing units, except when the first part of the name is not an English word, such as the Los in Los Angeles.

23. Titles or degrees of individuals, whether preceding or following the name, are not considered in indexing or filing. They are placed in parentheses after the given name or initial. Terms that designate seniority, such as Jr., Sr., 2d, are also placed in parentheses and are considered for indexing and filing only when the names to be indexed are otherwise identical.

    Exception A:

    When the name of an individual consists of a title and one name only, such as Queen Elizabeth, it is not transposed and the title is considered for indexing and filing.

    Exception B:

    When a title or foreign article is the initial word of a firm or association name, it is considered for indexing and filing.

24. Possessives

    When a word ends in apostrophe s, the s is not considered in indexing and filing. However, when a word ends in s apostrophe, because the s is part of the original word, it is considered. This rule is sometimes stated, "Consider everything up to the apostrophe. "

25. United States and foreign government names

    Names pertaining to the federal government are indexed and filed under United States Government and then subdivided by title of the department, bureau, division, commission, or board. Names pertaining to foreign governments are indexed and filed under names of countries and then subdivided by title of the department, bureau, division, commission, or board. Phrases, such as department of, bureau of, division of, commission of, board of, when used in titles of governmental bodies, are placed in parentheses after the word they modify, but are disregarded in indexing and filing. Such phrases, however, are considered in indexing and filing nongovernmental names.

26. Other political subdivisions

    Names pertaining to other political subdivisions, such as states, counties, cities, or towns, are indexed and filed under the name of the political subdivision and then subdivided by the title of the department, bureau, division, commission, or board.

27. Addresses

    When the same name appears with different addresses, the names are indexed as usual and arranged alphabetically according to city or town. The State is considered only when there is duplication of both individual or company name and city name. If the same name is located at different addresses within the same city, then the names are arranged alphabetically by streets. If the same name is located at more than one address on the same street, then the names are arranged from the lower to the higher street number.

28. Numbers

    Any number in a name is considered as though it were written in words, and it is indexed and filed as one unit.

29. Bank names

Because the names of many banking institutions are alike in several respects, as first National Bank, Second National Bank, etc., banks are indexed and filed first by city location, then by bank name, with the state location written in parentheses and considered only if necessary

30. Married women

The legal name of a married woman is the one used for filing purposes. Legally, a man's surname is the only part of a man's name a woman assumes when she marries. Her legal name, therefore, could be either:

(1) Her own first and middle names together with her husband's surname, or

(2) Her own first name and maiden surname, together with her husband's surname.

Mrs. is placed in parentheses at the end of the name. Her husband's first and middle names are given in parentheses below her legal name.

31. An alphabetically arranged list of names illustrating many difficult points of alphabetizing follows.

COLUMN I	COLUMN II
Abbot , W.B.	54th St. Tailor Shop
Abbott, Alice	Forstall, W.J.
Allen, Alexander B.	44th St. Garage
Allen, Alexander B., Inc.	M A Delivery Co.
Andersen, Hans	M & C Amusement Corp.
Andersen, Hans E.	M C Art Assn.
Andersen, Hans E., Jr.	MacAdam, Wm.
Anderson, Andrew Andrews,	Macaulay, James
George Brown Motor Co., Boston	MacAulay, Wilson
Brown Motor Co., Chicago	MacDonald, R.J.
Brown Motor Co., Philadelphia	Macdonald, S.B.
Brown Motor Co., San Francisco	Mace, Wm.
Dean, Anna	Mazza, Anthony
Dean, Anna F.	McAdam, Wm.
Dean, Anna Frances	McAndrews, Jerry
Dean & Co.	Meade & Clark Co.
Deane-Arnold Apartments	Meade, S.T.
Deane's Pharmacy	Meade, Solomon
Deans, Felix A.	Sackett Publishing Co.
Dean's Studio	Sacks, Robert
Deans, Wm.	St.Andrew Hotel
Deans & Williams	St.John, Homer W.
East Randolph	Saks, Isaac B.
East St.Louis	Stephens, Ira
Easton, Pa.	Stevens, Delevan
Eastport, Me.	Stevens, Delila

IV. OFFICIAL EXAMINATION DIRECTIONS AND RULES

To preclude the possibility of conflicting or varying methods of filing, explicit directions and express rules are given to the candidate before he answers the filing questions on an examination.

The most recent official directions and rules for the filing questions are given immediately hereafter.

OFFICIAL DIRECTIONS

Each of questions ... to ... consists of four(five)names. For each question, select the one of the four(five)names that should be first (second)(third)(last) if the four(five)names were arranged in alphabetical order in accordance with the rules for alphabetical filing given below. Read these rules carefully. Then, for each question, indicate in the correspondingly numbered row on the answer sheet the letter preceding the name that should be first(second)(third)(last) in alphabetical order.

OFFICIAL RULES FOR ALPHABETICAL FILING

Names of Individuals

1. The names of individuals are filed in strict alphabetical order, first according to the last name, then according to first name or initial, and, finally, according to middle name or initial. For example: William Jones precedes George Kirk and Arthur S. Blake precedes Charles M. Blake.
2. When the last names are identical, the one with an initial instead of a first name precedes the one "with a first name beginning with the same initial. For example: J.Green precedes Joseph Green.
3. When identical last names also have identical first names, the one without a middle name or initial precedes the one with a middle name or initial. For example:Robert Jackson precedes both Robert C.Jackson and Robert Chester Jackson.
4. When last names are identical and the first names are also identical, the one with a middle initial precedes the one with a middle name beginning with the same initial. For example: Peter A. Brown precedes Peter Alvin Brown.
5. Prefixes such as De, El, La, and Van are considered parts of the names they precede. For example:Wilfred DeWald precedes Alexander Duval.
6. Last names beginning with "Mac" or "Mc" are filed as spelled.
7. Abbreviated names are treated as if they were spelled out. For example: Jos. is filed as Joseph and Robt. is filed as Robert.
8. Titles and designations such as Dr. ,Mrs., Prof. are disregarded in filing.

Names of Business Organizations

1. The names of business organizations are filed exactly as written, except that an organization bearing the name of an individual is filed alphabetically according to the name of the individual in accordance with the rules for filing names of individuals given above. For example: Thomas Allison Machine Company precedes Northern Baking Company.
2. When numerals occur in a name, they are treated as if they were spelled out. For example: 6 stands for six and 4th stands for fourth.
3. When the following words occur in names, they are disregarded: the, of, and Sample: Choose the name that should be filed *third*.

(A) Fred Town	(2)	(C) D. Town	(1)
(B) Jack Towne	(3)	(D) Jack S.Towne	(4)

The numbers in parentheses indicate the proper alphabetical order in which these names should be filed. Since the name that should be filed <u>third</u> is Jack Towne, the answer is (B).

————

FILING

EXAMINATION SECTION
TEST 1

DIRECTIONS: Each of the following questions contains four names. For each question, choose the name that should be *FIRST* if the four names are to be arranged in alphabetical order in accordance with the Rules for Alphabetical Filing given before. Read these rules carefully. Then, for each question, indicate in the space at the right the letter before the name that should be *FIRST* in alphabetical order.

SAMPLE QUESTION
A.	Jane Earl	(2)
B.	James A. Earle	(4)
C.	James Earl	(1)
D.	J. Earle	(3)

The numbers in parentheses show the proper alphabetical order in which these names should be filed. Since the name that should be filed *FIRST* is James Earl, the answer to the Sample Question is C.

1.   A. Majorca Leather Goods   1._____
       B. Robert Maiorca and Sons
       C. Maintenance Management Corp.
       D. Majestic Carpet Mills

2.   A. Municipal Telephone Service   2._____
       B. Municipal Reference Library
       C. Municipal Credit Union
       D. Municipal Broadcasting System

3.   A. Robert B. Pierce   B. R. Bruce Pierce   3._____
       C. Ronald Pierce   D. Robert Bruce Pierce

4.   A. Four Seasons Sports Club   4._____
       B. 14 Street Shopping Center
       C. Forty Thieves Restaurant
       D. 42nd St. Theaters

5.   A. Franco Franceschini   B. Amos Franchini   5._____
       C. Sandra Franceschia   D. Lilie Franchinesca

KEY (CORRECT ANSWERS)

1. C
2. D
3. B
4. D
5. C

———

TEST 2

DIRECTIONS: Same as for Test 1.

1. A. Alan Carson, M. D.
    B. The Andrew Carlton Nursing Home
    C. Prof., Alfred P. Carlton
    D. Mr. A. Peter Carlton

    1.____

2. A. Chas. A. Denner   B. H. Jeffrey Dener
    C. Charles Denner   D. Harold Dener

    2.____

3. A. James C. Maziola   B. Joseph A. Mazzola
    C. James Maziola   D. J. Alfred Mazzola

    3.____

4. A. Bureau of Family Affairs
    B. Office of the Comptroller
    C. Department of Gas & Electricity
    D. Board of Estimate

    4.____

5. A. Robert Alan Pearson   B. John Charles Pierson
    C. Robert Allen Pearson   D. John Chester Pierson

    5.____

6. A. The Johnson Manufacturing Co.
    B. C. J. Johnston
    C. Bernard Johnsen
    D. Prof. Corey Johnstone

    6.____

7. A. Ninteenth Century Book Shop
    B. Ninth Federal Bank
    C. 19th Hole Coffee Shop
    D. 92nd St. Station

    7.____

8. A. George S. McNeely   B. Hugh J. Macintosh
    C. Mr. G. Stephen McNeally D. Mr. H. James Macintosh

    8.____

KEY (CORRECT ANSWERS)

1. D
2. B
3. C
4. B
5. A

6. C
7. A
8. D

TEST 3

DIRECTIONS: Each of the following questions consists of four names. For each question, choose the one of the four names that should be *LAST* if the four names were arranged in alphabetical order in accordance with the Rules for Alphabetical Filing given before. Read these rules carefully. Then, for each question, indicate in the space at the right the letter before the name that should be *LAST* in alphabetical order.

SAMPLE QUESTION.

A.	Jane Earl	(2)
B.	James A. Earle	(4)
C.	James Earl	(1)
D.	J. Earle	(3)

The numbers in parentheses show the proper alphabetical order in which these names should be filed. Since the name that should be filed *LAST* is James A. Earle, the answer to the Sample Question is B.

1.   A.   Steiner, Michael   B.   Steinblau, Dr. Walter   1.____
       C.   Steinet, Gary   D.   Stein, Prof. Edward

2.   A.   The Paper Goods Warehouse   2.____
       B.   T. Pane and Sons Inc.
       C.   Paley, Wallace
       D.   Painting Supplies Inc.

3.   A.   D'Angelo, F.   B.   De Nove, C.   3.____
       C.   Daniels, Frank   D.   Dovarre, Carl

4.   A.   Berene, Arnold   B.   Berene, Arnold L.   4.____
       C.   Beren, Arnold Lee   D.   Berene, A.

5.   A.   Kallinski, Liza   B.   Kalinsky, L.   5.____
       C.   Kallinky, E.   D.   Kallinsky, Elizabeth

6.   A.   Morgeno, Salvatore   6.____
       B.   Megan, J.
       C.   J. Morgenthal Consultant Services
       D.   Morgan, Janet

7.   A.   Ritter, G.   B.   Ritter, George   7.____
       C.   Riter, George H.   D.   Ritter, G. H.

8.   A.   Wheeler, Adele N.   B.   Wieler, Ada   8.____
       C.   Weiler, Adelaide   D.   Wheiler, Adele

9.   A.   Macan, Toby   B.   Maccini, T.   9.____
       C.   MacAvoy, Thomas   D.   Mackel, Theodore

10.   A.   Loomus, Kenneth   10._____
      B.   Lomis Paper Supplies
      C.   Loo, N.
      D.   Loomis Machine Repair Company

KEY (CORRECT ANSWERS)

1.   C
2.   A
3.   D
4.   B
5.   D

6.   C
7.   B
8.   B
9.   D
10. A

TEST 4

DIRECTIONS: In the following questions there are five notations numbered 1 through 5 shown in Column I. Each notation is made up of a supplier's name, a contract number, and a date and is to be filed according to the following rules:

First: File in alphabetical order.

Second: When two or more notations have the same supplier, file according to the contract number in numerical order beginning with the lowest number.

Third: When two or more notations have the same supplier and contract number, file according to the date beginning with the earliest date.

In Column II the lumbers 1 through 5 are arranged in four ways to show different possible orders in which the merchandise information might be filed. Pick the answer (A, B, C, or D) in Column II in which the notations are arranged according to the above filing rules.

SAMPLE QUESTION

Column I			Column II
1. Cluney	(4865)	6/17/72	A. 2, 3, 4, 1, 5
2. Roster	(2466)	5/10/71	B. 2, 5, 1, 3, 4
3. Altool	(7114)	10/15/72	C. 3, 2, 1, 4, 5
4. Cluney	(5276)	12/18/71	D. 3, 5, 1, 4, 2
5. Cluney	(4865)	4/8/72	

The *correct* way to file the notations is:

3.	Altool	(7114)	10/15/72
5.	Cluney	(4865)	4/8/72
1.	Cluney	(4865)	6/17/72
4.	Cluney	(5276)	12/18/71
2.	Roster	(2466)	5/10/71

The correct filing order is shown by the numbers in front of each name (3, 5, 1, 4, 2). The answer to the Sample Question is the letter in Column II in front of the numbers 3, 5, 1, 4, 2. This answer is D.

Column I	Column II	
1. 1. Fenten (38511) 1/4/73 2. Meadowlane (5020) 11/1/72 3. Whitehall (36142) 6/22/72 4. Clinton (4141) 5/26/71 5. Mester (8006) 4/20/71	A. 3, 5, 2, 1, 4 B. 4, 1, 2, 5, 3 C. 4, 2, 5, 3, 1 D. 5, 4, 3, 1, 2	1._____
2. 1. Harvard (2286) 2/19/70 2. Parker (1781) 4/12/72 3. Lenson (9044) 6/6/72 4. Brothers (38380) 10/11/72 5. Parker (41400) 12/20/70	A. 2, 4, 3, 1, 5 B. 2, 1, 3, 4, 5 C. 4, 1, 3, 2, 5 D. 5, 2, 3, 1, 4	2._____

3. 1. Newtone (3197) 8/22/70   A. 1, 4, 2, 5, 3   3.____
   2. Merritt (4071) 8/8/72   B. 4, 2, 1, 5, 3
   3. Writebest (60666) 4/7/71   C. 4, 5, 2, 1, 3
   4. Maltons (34380) 3/30/72   D. 5, 2, 4, 3, 1
   5. Merrit (4071) 7/16/71

4. 1. Weinburt (45514) 6/4/71   A. 4, 5, 2, 1, 3   4.____
   2. Owntye (35860) 10/4/72   B. 4, 2, 5, 3, 1
   3. Weinburt (45514) 2/1/72   C. 4, 2, 5, 1, 3
   4. Fasttex (7677) 11/10/71   D. 4, 5, 2, 3, 1
   5. Owntye (4574) 7/17/72

5. 1. Premier (1003) 7/29/70   A. 2, 1, 4, 3, 5   5.____
   2. Phylson (0031) 5/5/72   B. 3, 5, 4, 1, 2
   3. Lathen (3328) 10/3/71   C. 4, 1, 2, 3, 5
   4. Harper (8046) 8/18/72   D. 4, 3, 5, 2, 1
   5. Lathen (3328) 12/1/72

6. 1. Repper (46071) 10/14/72   A. 3, 2, 4, 5, 1   6.____
   2. Destex (77271) 8/27/72   B. 3, 4, 2, 5, 1
   3. Clawson (30736) 7/28/71   C. 3, 4, 5, 2, 1
   4. Destex (27207) 8/17/71   D. 3, 5, 4, 2, 1
   5. Destex (77271) 4/14/71

KEY (CORRECT ANSWERS)

   1. B
   2. C
   3. C
   4. A
   5. D
   6. C

TEST 5

DIRECTIONS: Each of the following questions repre-sents five cards to be filed, numbered 1 through 5 shown in Column I. Each card is made up of the employee's name, a work assignment code number shown in parentheses, and the date of this assignment. The cards are to be filed according to the following rules:

First: File in alphabetical order.

Second: When two or more cards have the same employee's name, file according to the work assignment number beginning with the lowest number.

Third: When two or more cards have the same employee's name and same assignment number, file according to the as-signment date beginning with the earliest date.

Column II shows the cards arranged in four different orders. Pick the answer (A, B, C, or D) in Column II which shows the cards arranged correctly according to the above filing rules.

SAMPLE QUESTION: See Sample Question (with answer) for Test 4.

Now answer the following questions according to these rules.

	Column I			Column II		
1.	1. Prichard	(013469)	4/6/71	A.	5, 4, 3, 2, 1	1.____
	2. Parks	(678941)	2/7/71	B.	1, 2, 5, 3, 4	
	3. Williams	(551467)	3/6/70	C.	2, 1, 5, 3, 4	
	4. Wilson	(551466)	8/9/67	D.	1, 5, 4, 3, 2	
	5. Stanhope	(300014)	8/9/67			
2.	1. Ridgeway	(623809)	8/11/71	A.	5, 1, 3, 4, 2	2.____
	2. Travers	(305439)	4/5/67	B.	5, 1, 3, 2, 4	
	3. Tayler	(818134)	7/5/68	C.	1, 5, 3, 2, 4	
	4. Travers	(305349)	5/6/70	D.	1, 5, 4, 2, 3	
	5. Ridgeway	(623089)	10/9/71			
3.	1. Jaffe	(384737)	2/19/71	A.	3, 5, 2, 4, 1	3.____
	2. Inez	(859176)	8/8/72	B.	3, 5, 2, 1, 4	
	3. Ingrahm	(946460)	8/6/69	C.	2, 3, 5, 1, 4	
	4. Karp	(256146)	5/5/70	D.	2, 3, 5, 4, 1	
	5. Ingrahm	(946460)	6/4/70			
4.	1. Marrano	(369421)	7/24/69	A.	1, 5, 3, 4, 2	4.____
	2. Marks	(652910)	2/23/71	B.	3, 5, 4, 2, 1	
	3. Netto	(556772)	3/10/72	C.	2, 4, 1, 5, 3	
	4. Marks	(652901)	2/17/72	D.	4, 2, 1, 5, 3	
	5. Netto	(556772)	6/17/70			

5. 1. Abernathy (712467) 6/23/70   A. 5, 3, 1, 2, 4   5.____
    2. Acevedo   (680262) 6/23/68   B. 5, 4, 2, 3, 1
    3. Aaron   (967647) 1/17/69   C. 1, 3, 5, 2, 4
    4. Acevedo   (680622) 5/14/67   D. 2, 4, 1, 5, 3
    5. Aaron   (967647) 4/1/65

6. 1. Simon   (645219) 8/19/70   A. 4, 1, 2, 5, 3   6.____
    2. Simon   (645219) 9/2/68   B. 4, 5, 2, 1, 3
    3. Simons   (645218) 7/7/70   C. 3, 5, 2, 1, 4
    4. Simms   (646439) 10/12/71   D. 5, 1, 2, 3, 4
    5. Simon   (645219) 10/16/67

7. 1. Rappaport (312230) 6/11/71   A. 4, 3, 1, 2, 5   7.____
    2. Rascio   (777510) 2/9/70   B. 4, 3, 1, 5, 2
    3. Rappaport (312230) 7/3/67   C. 3, 4, 1, 5, 2
    4. Rapaport   (312330) 9/6/70   D. 5, 2, 4, 3, 1
    5. Rascio   (777501) 7/7/70

8. 1. Johnson   (843250) 6/8/67   A. 1, 3, 2, 4, 5   8.____
    2. Johnson   (843205) 4/3/70   B. 1, 3, 2, 5, 4
    3. Johnson   (843205) 8/6/67   C. 3, 2, 1, 4, 5
    4. Johnson   (843602) 3/8/71   D. 3, 2, 1, 5, 4
    5. Johnson   (843602) 8/3/70

KEY (CORRECT ANSWERS)

1. C
2. A
3. C
4. D
5. A

6. B
7. B
8. D

TEST 6

DIRECTIONS: In each of the following questions there are four groups of names. One of the groups in each question is *NOT* in correct alphabetic order. Mark the letter of that group next to the number that corresponds to the number of the question.

1.   A. Ace Advertising Agency; Acel, Erwin; Ad Graphics; Ade, E. J. & Co.
     B. Advertising Bureau, Inc.; Advertising Guild, Inc.; Advertising Ideas, Inc.; Advertising Sales Co.
     C. Allan Associates; Allen-Wayne, Inc.; Alley & Richards, Inc.; Allum, Ralph
     D. Anderson & Cairnes; Amos Parrish & Co.; Anderson Merrill Co.; Anderson, Milton

1.____

2.   A. Bach, Henry; Badillo, John; Baer, Budd; Bair, Albert
     B. Baker, Lynn; Bakers, Albert; Bailin, Henry; Bakers Franchise Corp.
     C. Bernhardt, Manfred; Bernstein, Jerome; Best, Frank; Benton Associates
     D. Brandford, Edward; Branstatter Associates; Brown, Martel; Browne, Bert

2.____

3.   A. Cone, Robert; Contempo, Bernard; Conti Advertising; Cooper, James
     B. Cramer, Zed; Creative Sales; Crofton, Ada; Cromwell, Samuel
     C. Cheever, Fred; Chernow Advertising; Chenault Associates; Chesler, Arthur
     D. Chain Store Advertising; Chair Lawrence & Co.; Chaite, Alexander E.; Chase, Luis

3.____

4.   A. Delahanty, Francis; Dela McCarthy Associates; Dele- hanty, Kurnit; Delroy, Stewart
     B. Doerfler, B. R.; Doherty, Clifford; Dorchester Apartments; Dorchester, Monroe
     C. Drayer, Stella; Dreher, Norton; Dreyer, Harvey; Dryer, Lester
     D. Duble, Normal; Duevell, William C.; Du Fine, August; Dugan, Harold

4.____

5.   A. Esmond, Walter; Esty, Willia; Ettinger, Carl; Everett, Austin
     B. Enlos, Cartez; Entertainment, Inc.; Englemore, Irwin; Equity Associates
     C. Einhorn, Anna Mrs.; Einhorn, Arlene; Eisele, Mary; Eisele, Minnie Mrs.
     D. Eagen, Roy; Egale, George; Egan, Barrett; Eisen, Henry

5.____

6.   A. Funt-Rand Inc.; Furman, Fainer & Co.; Furman Roth & Co.; Fusco, Frank A.
     B. Friedan, Phillip; Friedman, Mitchell; Friend, Harvey; Friend, Herbert
     C. Folkart Greeting Cards; Food Service; Foote, Cornelius; Foreign Advertising
     D. Finkels, Eliot; Finnerman, John; Finneran, Joseph; Fire-stone, Albert

6.____

7. A. Gubitz, Jay; Guild, Dorothy; Gumbiner, B.; Gussow, Leonard
    B. Gore, Smith; Gotham Art, Inc.; Gotham Editors Service; Gotham-Vladimir, Inc.
    C. Georgian, Wolf; Gerdts, H. J.; German News Co.; Germaine, Werner
    D. Gardner, Fred; Gardner, Roy; Garner, Roy; Gaynor & Ducal, Inc.

7.____

8. A. Howard, E. T.; Howard, Francis; Howson, Allen; Hoyt, Charles
    B. Houston, Byron; House of Graphics; Rowland, Lynne; Hoyle, Mortimer
    C. Hi-Lite Art Service; Hickerson, J. M.; Hickey, Murphy Hicks, Gilbert
    D. Hyman, Bram; Hyman, Charles B.; Hyman, Claire; Hyman, Claude

8.____

9. A. Idone, Leopold; Ingraham, Evelyn; Ianuzzi, Frank; Itkin, Simon
    B. Ideas, Inc.; Inter-Racial Press, Inc.; International Association; Iverson, Ford
    C. Il Trionofo; Inwood Bake Shop; Iridor, Rose; Italian Pastry
    D. Ionadi, Anthony; Irena, Louise; Iris, Ysabella; Isabelle, Arlia

9.____

10. A. Jonas, Myron; Johnstone, John; Jones, Julius; Joptha, Meyer
    B. Jeanne's Beauty Shoppe; Jeger, Jans; Jem, H.; Jim's Grill
    C. Jacobs, Abraham & Co.; Jacobs, Harold A.; Jacobs, Joseph; Jacobs, M. J.
    D. Japan Air Lines; Jensen, Arne; Judson, P.; Juliano, Jeremiah

10.____

KEY (CORRECT ANSWERS)

1. D
2. B
3. C
4. A
5. B

6. D
7. C
8. B
9. A
10. A

TEST 7

DIRECTIONS: Below are ten groups of names, numbered 1 through 10. For each group, three different filing arrangements of the names in the group are given. In only *ONE* of these arrangements are the names in correct filing order according to standard rules for filing. For each group, select the *ONE* arrangement, lettered A, B, C, that is *CORRECT*.

1. *Arrangement A*
Nichols, C. Arnold
Nichols, Bruce
Nicholson, Arthur

Arrangement B
Nichols, Bruce
Nichols, C. Arnold
Nicholson, Arthur

1.____

Arrangement C
Nicholson, Arthur
Nichols, Bruce
Nichols, C. Arnold

2. *Arrangement A*
Schaefer's Drug Store
Schaefer, Harry T.
Schaefer Bros.

Arrangement B
Schaefer Bros.
Schaefer, Harry T.
Schaefer's Drug Store

2.____

Arrangement C
Schaefer Bros;
Schaefer's Drug Store
Schaefer, Harry T.

3. *Arrangement A*
Adams' Dime Store
Adami, David
Adams, Donald

Arrangement B
Adami, David
Adams' Dime Store
Adams, Donald

Arrangement C
Adami, David
Adams, Donald
Adams' Dime Store

3.____

4. *Arrangement A*
Newton, Jas. F.
Newton, Janet
Newton-Jarvis Law Firm

Arrangement B
Newton-Jarvis Law Firm
Newton, Jas. F.
Newton, Janet

4.____

Arrangement C
Newton, Janet
Newton-Jarvis Law Firm
Newton, Jas. F.

5. *Arrangement A*
Radford and Bigelow
Radford Transfer Co.
Radford-Smith, Albert

Arrangement B
Radford and Bigelow
Radford-Smith, Albert
Radford Transfer Co.

5.____

Arrangement C
Radford Transfer Co.
Radford and Bigelow
Radford-Smith, Albert

6. *Arrangement A*
   Trent, Inc.
   Trent Farm Products
   20th Century Film Corp.

   Arrangement B
   20th Century Film Corp.
   Trent Farm Products
   Trent, Inc.

   6.____

   Arrangement C
   Trent Farm Products
   Trent, Inc.
   20th Century Film Corp.

7. *Arrangement A*
   Morrell, Ralph
   M.R.B. Paper Co.
   Mt.Ranier Hospital

   Arrangement B
   Morrell, Ralph
   Mt.Ranier Hospital
   M.R.B. Paper Co.

   Arrangement C
   M.R.B. Paper Co.
   Morrell, Ralph
   Mt.Ranier Hospital

   7.____

8. *Arrangement A*
   Vanity Faire Shop
   Van Loon, Charles
   The Williams Magazine Corp.

   Arrangement B
   The Williams Magazine Corp.
   Van Loon, Charles
   Vanity Faire Shop

   8.____

   Arrangement C
   Van Loon, Charles
   Vanity Faire Shop
   The Williams Magazine Corp.

9. *Arrangement A*
   Crane and Jones Ins. Co.
   Little Folks Shop
   L. J. Coughtry Mfg. Co.

   Arrangement B
   L. J. Coughtry Mfg. Co.
   Crane and Jones Ins. Co.
   Little Folks Shop

   9.____

   Arrangement C
   Little Folks Shop
   L. J. Coughtry Mfg. Co.
   Crane and Jones Ins. Co.

10. *Arrangement A*
    South Arlington Garage
    N. Y. State Dept. of Audit and Control
    State Antique Shop

    Arrangement B
    N. Y. State Dept. of Audit and Control
    South Arlington Garage
    State Antique Shop

    10.____

    Arrangement C
    State Antique Shop
    South Arlington Garage
    N. Y. State Dept. of Audit and Control

KEY (CORRECT ANSWERS)

1. B
2. C
3. B
4. A
5. B

6. C
7. A
8. A
9. B
10. B

TEST 8

DIRECTIONS: Same as for Test 7.

1.   *Arrangement A*
    Gillilan, William
    Gililane, Ethel
    Gillihane, Harry

   Arrangement B
   Gililane, Ethel
   Gillihane, Harry
   Gillilan, William

   Arrangement C
   Gillihane, Harry
   Gillilan, William
   Gililane, Ethel

1.____

2.   Stevens, J.Donald
    Stevenson, David
    Stevens, James

   Stevenson, David
   Stevens, J.Donald
   Stevens, James

   Stevens, J.Donald
   Stevens, James
   Stevenson, David

2.____

3.   Brooks, Arthur E.
    Brooks, H.Albert
    Brooks, H.T.

   Brooks, H.T.
   Brooks. H.Albert
   Brooks. Arthur E.

   Brooks, H.Albert
   Brooks, Arthur E.
   Brooks, H.T.

3.____

4.   *Arrangement A*
    Lafayette, Earl
    Le Grange, Wm. J.
    La Roux Haberdashery

   Arrangement C
   Lafayette, Earl
   La Roux Haberdashery
   Le Grange, Wm. J.

   Arrangement B
   Le Grange, Wm. J.
   La Roux Haberdashery
   Lafayette, Earl

4.____

5.   *Arrangement A*
    Mosher Bros.
    Mosher's Auto Repair
    Mosher, Dorothy

   Arrangement C
   Mosher Bros.
   Mosher, Dorothy
   Mosher's Auto Repair

   Arrangement B
   Mosher's Auto Repair
   Mosher Bros.
   Mosher, Dorothy

5.____

6.   *Arrangement A*
    Ainsworth, Inc.
    Ainsworth,George
    Air-O-Pad Co.

   Arrangement B
   Ainsworth, George
   Ainsworth, Inc.
   Air-O-Pad Co.

   Arrangement C
   Air-O-Pad Co.
   Ainsworth, George
   Ainsworth, Inc.

6.____

7.   *Arrangement A*
    Peters' Printing Co.
    Peterbridge, Alfred
    Peters, Paul

   Arrangement C
   Peters, Paul
   Peters' Printing Co.
   Peterbridge, Alfred

   Arrangement B
   Peterbridge, Alfred
   Peters, Paul
   Peters' Printing Co.

7.____

8. *Arrangement A*
Sprague-Miller, Ella
Sprague (and) Reed
Sprague Insurance Co.

Arrangement C
Sprague Insurance Co.
Sprague (and) Reed
Sprague-Miller, Ella

Arrangement B
Sprague (and) Reed
Sprague Insurance Co.
Sprague-Miller, Ella

8.____

9. *Arrangement A*
Ellis, Chalmers Adv. Agency
Ellis, Chas.
Ellis, Charlotte

Arrangement C
Ellis, Charlotte
Ellis, Chas.
Ellis, Chalmers Adv. Agency

Arrangement B
Ellis, Chas.
Ellis, Charlotte
Ellis, Chalmers Adv. Agency

9.____

10. *Arrangement A*
Adams, Paul
Five Acres Coffee Shop
Fielding Adjust. Co.

Arrangement C
Adams, Paul
Fielding Adjust. Co.
Five Acres Coffee Chop

Arrangement B
Five Acres Coffee Shop
Adams, Paul
Fielding Adjust. Co.

10.____

KEY (CORRECT ANSWERS)

1.	B
2.	C
3.	A
4.	C
5.	B
6.	B
7.	B
8.	C
9.	A
10.	C

TEST 9

DIRECTIONS: Below in Section A is a diagram representing 40 divisional drawers in alphabetic file, numbered 1 through 40. Below in Section B is a list of 30 names to be filed, numbered 1 through 30, with a drawer number opposite each name, representing the drawer in which it is assumed a file clerk has filed the name.

Determine which are filed *CORRECTLY* and which are filed *INCORRECTLY* based on standard rules for indexing and filing. If the name is filed *CORRECTLY*, print in the space at the right the letter C. If the name is filed *INCORRECTLY*, print in the space at the right the letter I.

SECTION A

1 Aa-Al	6 Bs-Bz	11 Ea-Er	16 Gp-Gz	21 Kp-Kz	26 Mo-Mz	31 Qa-Qz	36 Ta-Ti
2 Am-Au	7 Ca-Ch	12 Es-Ez	17 Ha-Hz	22 La-Le	27 Na-Nz	32 Ra-Rz	37 Tj-Tz
3 Av-Az	8 Ci-Co	13 Fa-Fr	18 Ia-Iz	23 Lf-Lz	28 Oa-Oz	33 Sa-Si	38 U-V
4 Ba-Bi	9 Cp-Cz	14 Fa-Fz	19 Ja-Jz	24 Ma-Mi	29 Pa-Pr	34 Sj-St	39 Wa-Wz
5 Bj-Br	10 Da-Dz	15 Ga-Go	20 Ka-Ko	25 Mj-Mo	30 Ps-Pz	35 Su-Sz	40 X-Y-Z

SECTION B

	Name or Title	Drawer No.	
1.	William O'Dea	28	1._____
2.	J. Arthur Crawford	8	2._____
3.	DuPont Chemical Co.	10	3._____
4.	Arnold Bros. Mfg. Co.	2	4._____
5.	Dr. Charles Ellis	10	5._____
6.	Gray and Doyle Adv. Agency	16	6._____
7.	Tom's Smoke Shop	37	7._____
8.	Wm. E. Jarrett Motor Corp.	39	8._____
9.	Penn-York Air Service	29	9._____
10.	Corinne La Fleur	13	10._____
11.	Cartright, Incorporated	7	11._____
12.	7th Ave. Market	24	12._____
13.	Ft.Schuyler Apts.	13	13._____
14.	Madame Louise	23	14._____

15.	Commerce Dept., U. S. Govt.	38	15.____
16.	Norman Bulwer-Lytton	6	16.____
17.	Hilton Memorial Library	17	17.____
18.	The Linen Chest Gift Shop	36	18.____
19.	Ready Mix Supply Co.	32	19.____
20.	City Service Taxi	8	20.____
21.	A.R.C. Transportation Co.	37	21.____
22.	New Jersey Insurance Co.	19	22.____
23.	Capt. Larry Keith	20	23.____
24.	Girl Scouts Council	15	24.____
25.	University of Michigan	24	25.____
26.	Sister Ursula	38	26.____
27.	Am. Legion Post #9	22	27.____
28.	Board of Hudson River Reg. Dist.	17	28.____
29.	Mid West Bus Lines	39	29.____
30.	South West Tours, Inc.	34	30.____

———

KEY (CORRECT ANSWERS)

1.	C	16.	C
2.	I	17.	C
3.	C	18.	I
4.	C	19.	C
5.	I	20.	C
6.	C	21.	I
7.	C	22.	I
8.	I	23.	C
9.	C	24.	C
10.	I	25.	I
11.	C	26.	I
12.	I	27.	I
13.	C	28.	C
14.	I	29.	I
15.	C	30.	C

TEST 10

DIRECTIONS: Each question or incomplete statement is followed by several suggested answers or completions. Select the one that BEST answers the question or completes the statement. *PRINT THE LETTER OF THE CORRECT ANSWER IN THE SPACE AT THE RIGHT.*

1. Of the following statements about the numeric system of filing, the one which is COR-RECT is that it   1._____

   A. is the least accurate of all methods of filing
   B. eliminates the need for cross-referencing
   C. allows for very limited expansion
   D. requires a separate index

2. When more than one name or subject is involved in a piece of correspondence to be filed, the office assistant should, *generally,*   2._____

   A. prepare a cross-reference sheet
   B. establish a geographical filing system
   C. prepare out-guides
   D. establish a separate index card file for noting such correspondence

3. A tickler file is MOST generally used for   3._____

   A. identification of material contained in a numeric file
   B. maintenance of a current listing of telephone numbers
   C. follow-up of matters requiring future attention
   D. control of records borrowed or otherwise removed from the file

4. In filing, the name Ms. "Ann Catalana-Moss" should *generally* be indexed as   4._____

   A. Moss, Catalana, Ann (Ms.)
   B. Catalana-Moss, Ann (Ms.)
   C. Ann Catalana-Moss (Ms.)
   D. Moss-Catalana, Ann (Ms.)

5. An office assistant has a set of four cards, each of which contains one of the following names. In alphabetic filing, the FIRST of the cards to be filed is   5._____

   A. (Ms.)Alma John
   B. Mrs. John (Patricia) Edwards
   C. John-Edward School Supplies, Inc.
   D. John H. Edwards

6. *Generally,* of the following, the name to be filed FIRST in an alphabetical filing system is   6._____

   A. Diane Maestro   B. Diana McElroy
   C. James Mackell   D. James McKell

7. According to *generally* recognized rules of filing in an alphabetic filing system, the one of the following names which normally should be filed LAST is   7._____

   A. Department of Education, New York State
   B. F. B. I.
   C. Police Department of New York City
   D. P. S. 81 of New York City

KEY (CORRECT ANSWERS)

1. D
2. A
3. C
4. B
5. D
6. C
7. B

READING COMPREHENSION
UNDERSTANDING AND INTERPRETING WRITTEN MATERIAL
EXAMINATION SECTION
TEST 1

DIRECTIONS: Each question or incomplete statement is followed by several suggested answers or completions. Select the one that BEST answers the question or completes the statement. *PRINT THE LETTER OF THE CORRECT ANSWER IN THE SPACE AT THE RIGHT.*

Questions 1-6.

DIRECTIONS: Questions 1 through 6 are to be answered SOLELY on the basis of the information contained in the following passage.

Duplicating is the process of making a number of identical copies of letters, documents, etc from an original. Some duplicating processes make copies directly from the original document. Other duplicating processes require the preparation of a special master, and copies are then made from the master. Four of the most common duplicating processes are stencil, fluid, offset, and xerox.

In the stencil process, the typewriter is used to cut the words into a master called a stencil. Drawings, charts, or graphs can be cut into the stencil using a stylus. As many as 3,500 good-quality copies can be reproduced from one stencil. Various grades of finished paper from inexpensive mimeograph to expensive bond can be used.

The fluid process is a good method of copying from 50 to 125 good-quality copies from a master, which is prepared with a special dye. The master is placed on the duplicator, and special paper with a hard finish is moistened and then passed through the duplicator. Some of the dye on the master is dissolved, creating an impression on the paper. The impression becomes lighter as more copies are made; and once the dye on the master is used up, a new master must be made.

The offset process is the most adaptable office duplicating process because this process can be used for making a few copies or many copies. Masters can be made on paper or plastic for a few hundred copies, or on metal plates for as many as 75,000 copies. By using a special technique called photo-offset, charts, photographs, illustrations, or graphs can be reproduced on the master plate. The offset process is capable of producing large quantities of fine, top-quality copies on all types of finished paper.

The xerox process reproduces an exact duplicate from an original. It is the fastest duplicating method because the original material is placed directly on the duplicator, eliminating the need to make a special master. Any kind of paper can be used. The xerox process is the most expensive duplicating process; however, it is the best method of reproducing small quantities of good-quality copies of reports, letters, official documents, memos, or contracts.

1. Of the following, the MOST efficient method of reproducing 5,000 copies of a graph is   1.____

    A. stencil   B. fluid
    C. offset   D. Xerox

2. The offset process is the MOST adaptable office duplicating process because   2.____

    A. it is the quickest duplicating method
    B. it is the least expensive duplicating method
    C. it can produce a small number or large number of copies
    D. a softer master can be used over and over again

3. Which one of the following duplicating processes uses moistened paper?   3.____

    A. Stencil   B. Fluid
    C. Offset   D. Xerox

4. The fluid process would be the BEST process to use for reproducing   4.____

    A. five copies of a school transcript
    B. fifty copies of a memo
    C. five hundred copies of a form letter
    D. five thousand copies of a chart

5. Which one of the following duplicating processes does NOT require a special master?   5.____

    A. Fluid   B. Xerox
    C. Offset   D. Stencil

6. Xerox is NOT used for all duplicating jobs because   6.____

    A. it produces poor-quality copies
    B. the process is too expensive
    C. preparing the master is too time-consuming
    D. it cannot produce written reports

Questions 7-10.

DIRECTIONS: Questions 7 through 10 are to be answered SOLELY on the basis of the information contained in the following passage.

City government is committed to providing a safe and healthy work environment for all city employees. An effective agency safety program reduces accidents by educating employees about the types of careless acts which can cause accidents. Even in an office, accidents can happen. If each employee is aware of possible safety hazards, the number of accidents on the job can be reduced.

Careless use of office equipment can cause accidents and injuries. For example, file cabinet drawers which are filled with papers can be so heavy that the entire cabinet could tip over from the weight of one open drawer.

The bottom drawers of desks and file cabinets should never be left open since employees could easily trip over open drawers and injure themselves.

When reaching for objects on a high shelf, an employee should use a strong, sturdy object such as a step stool to stand on. Makeshift platforms made out of books, papers, or boxes can easily collapse. Even chairs can slide out from under foot, causing serious injury.

Even at an employee's desk, safety hazards can occur. Frayed or cut wires should be repaired or replaced immediately. Typewriters which are not firmly anchored to the desk or table could fall, causing injury.

Smoking is one of the major causes of fires in the office. A lighted match or improperly extinguished cigarette thrown into a wastebasket filled with paper could cause a major fire with possible loss of life. Where smoking is permitted, ashtrays should be used. Smoking is particularly dangerous in offices where flammable chemicals are used.

7. The goal of an effective safety program is to

    A. reduce office accidents
    B. stop employees from smoking on the job
    C. encourage employees to continue their education
    D. eliminate high shelves in offices

7.____

8. Desks and file cabinets can become safety hazards when

    A. their drawers are left open
    B. they are used as wastebaskets
    C. they are makeshift
    D. they are not anchored securely to the floor

8.____

9. Smoking is especially hazardous when it occurs

    A. near exposed wires
    B. in a crowded office
    C. in an area where flammable chemicals are used
    D. where books and papers are stored

9.____

10. Accidents are likely to occur when

    A. employees' desks are cluttered with books and papers
    B. employees are not aware of safety hazards
    C. employees close desk drawers
    D. step stools are used to reach high objects

10.____

Questions 11-18.

DIRECTIONS: Questions 11 through 18 are to be answered SOLELY on the basis of the information contained in the following passage.

The telephone directory is made up of two books. The first book consists of the introductory section and the alphabetical listing of names section. The second book is the classified directory (also known as the yellow pages). Many people who are familiar with one book do not realize how useful the other can be. The efficient office worker should become familiar with both books in order to make the best use of this important source of information.

The introductory section gives general instructions for finding numbers in the alphabetical listing and classified directory. This section also explains how to use the telephone company's many services, including the operator and information services, gives examples of charges for local and long distance calls, and lists area codes for the entire country. In addition, this section provides a useful postal zip code map.

The alphabetical listing of names section lists the names, addresses, and telephone numbers of subscribers in an area. Guide names, or *telltales*, are on the top corner of each page. These guide names indicate the first and last name to be found on that page. *Telltales* help locate any particular name quickly. A cross-reference spelling is also given to help locate names which are spelled several different ways. City, state, and federal government agencies are listed under the major government heading. For example, an agency of the federal government would be listed under *United States Government*.

The classified directory, or yellow pages, is a separate book. In this section are advertising services, public transportation line maps, shopping guides, and listings of businesses arranged by the type of product or services they offer. This book is most useful when looking for the name or phone number of a business when all that is known is the type of product offered and the address, or when trying to locate a particular type of business in an area. Businesses listed in the classified directory can usually be found in the alphabetical listing of names section. When the name of the business is known, you will find the address or phone number more quickly in the alphabetical listing of names section.

11. The introductory section provides   11._____

    A. shopping guides   B. government listings
    C. business listings   D. information services

12. Advertising services would be found in the   12._____

    A. introductory section
    B. alphabetical listing of names section
    C. classified directory
    D. information services

13. According to the information in the above passage for locating government agencies, the   13._____
Information Office of the Department of Consumer Affairs of New York City government
would be alphabetically listed FIRST under

    A. *I* for Information Offices
    B. *D* for Department of Consumer Affairs
    C. *N* for New York City
    D. *G* for government

14. When the name of a business is known, the QUICKEST way to find the phone number is   14._____
to look in the

    A. classified directory
    B. introductory section
    C. alphabetical listing of names section
    D. advertising service section

15. The QUICKEST way to find the phone number of a business when the type of service a   15.____
business offers and its address is known is to look in the

    A. classified directory
    B. alphabetical listing of names section
    C. introductory section
    D. information service

16. What is a *telltale*?   16.____
A(n)

    A. alphabetical listing   B. guide name
    C. map   D. cross-reference listing

17. The BEST way to find a postal zip code is to look in the   17.____

    A. classified directory
    B. introductory section
    C. alphabetical listing of names section
    D. government heading

18. To help find names which have several different spellings, the telephone directory pro-   18.____
vides

    A. cross-reference spelling
    B. *tell tales*
    C. spelling guides
    D. advertising services

Questions 19-24.

DIRECTIONS: Questions 19 through 24 are to be answered on the basis of the information
                       contained in the following instructions on

SWEEPING

All sweeping must be done with damp sawdust, which is used to prevent the raising of
dust when sweeping platforms and mezzanines. Soak sawdust thoroughly in a bucket of
water for two to three hours before use. Drain before use so that no stains are left on concrete
from excess water. In order to keep sawdust moist while being used, spread for an area of
120 feet in advance of actual sweeping. Never sweep sawdust over drains. To assure good
footing, do not spread it on stairways or on damp or wet floor areas.

19. Dampened sawdust should be used when   19.____

    A. scrapping   B. dusting
    C. sweeping   D. mopping

20. Of the following procedures, which is the CORRECT order to be followed when sweeping   20.____
with sawdust?

    A. Soak, drain, and spread   B. Spread, drain, and soak
    C. Spread, soak, and drain   D. Drain, spread, and soak

21. Of the following, it is MOST correct to soak the sawdust in a bucket of water for _____ hour(s).   21.____

    A. a half-hour to an   B. one to two
    C. two to three   D. three to four

22. The water should be drained from the bucket of sawdust so that excess water does NOT   22.____

    A. cause passengers to lose their footing
    B. stain the concrete
    C. flood the tracks
    D. slow down the sweeping

23. Sawdust is dampened in order to   23.____

    A. assure good footing on stairways
    B. prevent the raising of dust when sweeping
    C. prevent the staining of concrete
    D. cool off platforms

24. The dampened sawdust may be spread on   24.____

    A. wet floors   B. drains
    C. stairways   D. mezzanines

Questions 25-27.

DIRECTIONS: Questions 25 through 27 are to be answered on the basis of the information contained in the following paragraph.

Whether a main lobby or upper corridor requires scrubbing or mopping and whether it should be done nightly or less frequently depends on the nature of the floor surface and the amount of traffic. In a building with heavy traffic, it may be desirable every night to scrub the main lobby and to mop the upper floor corridors. In such cases, it may also be found desirable to scrub the upper floors once a week. If traffic is light, it may be only necessary to mop the main lobby every other night and to mop the upper floor corridors once a week. If there is any traffic or usage at all, it will be necessary to at least sweep the corridors nightly.

25. According to the above paragraph, in a building with light traffic, the upper floor corridors should be   25.____

    A. swept every other night
    B. mopped every night
    C. swept nightly
    D. mopped every other night

26. According to the above paragraph, the number of times a floor is cleaned depends   26.____

    A. mainly on the type of floor surface
    B. mainly on the type of traffic
    C. only on the amount of traffic
    D. on both the floor surface and amount of traffic

27. According to the above paragraph, it may be DESIRABLE to have a heavily used main lobby swept   27.____

    A. daily and scrubbed weekly
    B. daily and mopped weekly
    C. and mopped weekly
    D. and scrubbed daily

Questions 28-30.

DIRECTIONS: Questions 28 through 30 are to be answered SOLELY on the basis of the information contained in the passage below.

SENIOR CITIZEN AND HANDICAPPED PASSENGER REDUCED FARE PROGRAM

Upon display of his or her Medicare Card, Senior Citizen Reduced Fare Card, or Handicapped Photo I.D. Card to the Railroad Clerk on duty, and upon purchase of a token or evidence of having a token, a passenger will be issued a free return trip ticket. The passenger will then be directed to deposit full fare in a turnstile and enter the controlled area. Return trip tickets are valid 24 hours a day, 7 days a week, for the day of purchase and the following two (2) calendar days.

Each return trip ticket will be stamped with the station name and the date only at the time of issuing to a properly identified senior citizen or handicapped passenger. Overstamping of tickets is not allowed. Return trip tickets issued from 2300 hours will be stamped with the date of the following day.

On the return trip, the Railroad Clerk on duty will direct the passenger to enter the controlled area via the exit gate upon the passenger turning in the return trip ticket and displaying his/her Medicare Card, Senior Citizen Reduced Fare Card, or Handicapped Photo I.D. Card.

28. A Railroad Clerk issued a free return ticket to a senior citizen who displayed a birth certificate and a token. The Railroad Clerk's action was   28.____

    A. *proper* because the Railroad Clerk had proof of the senior citizen's age
    B. *improper* because the senior citizen did not display a Medicare Card, Senior Citizen Reduced Fare Card, or Handicapped Photo I.D. Card
    C. *proper* because it is inconvenient for many senior citizens to obtain a Medicare Card, Senior Citizen Reduced Fare Card, or Handicapped Photo I.D. Card
    D. *improper* because the senior citizen did not buy a token from the Railroad Clerk

29. The return trip ticket issued to a senior citizen is valid for ONLY   29.____

    A. 24 hours
    B. the day of purchase
    C. two days
    D. the day of purchase and the following two calendar days

30. A Railroad Clerk denied entry to the controlled area via the exit gate to an 18 year-old handicapped passenger who turned in a correctly stamped return trip ticket, but did not display any type of identification card. The Railroad Clerk's action was

30.____

   A. *proper* because the passenger should have displayed his Handicapped Photo I.D. Card
   B. *improper* because the passenger turned in a correctly stamped return trip ticket
   C. *proper* because the passenger should have displayed either his Handicapped Photo I.D. Card or Social Security Card
   D. *improper* because it should have been obvious to the Railroad Clerk that the passenger was handicapped

---

KEY (CORRECT ANSWERS)

1.	C	16.	B
2.	C	17.	B
3.	B	18.	A
4.	B	19.	C
5.	B	20.	A
6.	A	21.	C
7.	A	22.	B
8.	A	23.	B
9.	C	24.	D
10.	B	25.	C
11.	D	26.	D
12.	C	27.	D
13.	C	28.	B
14.	C	29.	D
15.	A	30.	A

TEST 2

DIRECTIONS: Each question or incomplete statement is followed by several suggested answers or completions. Select the one that BEST answers the question or completes the statement. *PRINT THE LETTER OF THE CORRECT ANSWER IN THE SPACE AT THE RIGHT.*

Questions 1-2.

DIRECTIONS: Questions 1 and 2 are to be answered on the basis of the information given in the following passage.

The Commissioner of Investigation shall have general responsibility for the investigation and elimination of corrupt or other criminal activity, conflicts of interest, unethical conduct, misconduct, and incompetence by city agencies, by city officers and employees, and by persons regulated by, doing business with, or receiving funds directly or indirectly from the city, with respect to their dealings with the city. All agency heads shall be responsible for establishing, subject to review for completeness and inter-agency consistency by the Commissioner of Investigation, written standards of conduct for the officials and employees of their respective agencies, and fair and efficient disciplinary systems to maintain those standards of conduct. All agencies shall have an Inspector General who shall report directly to the respective agency head and to the Commissioner of Investigation and be responsible for maintaining standards of conduct as may be established in such agency under this Order. Inspectors General shall be responsible for the investigation and elimination of corrupt or other criminal activity, conflicts of interest, unethical conduct, misconduct, and incompetence within their respective agencies. Except to the extent otherwise provided by law, the employment or continued employment of all existing and prospective Inspectors General and members of their staffs shall be subject to complete background investigations and approval by the Department of Investigation.

1. According to the above passage, establishing written standards of conduct for each agency is the responsibility of the   1.____

   A. agency head
   B. Commissioner of Investigation
   C. Department of Investigation
   D. Inspector General

2. According to the above passage, maintaining standards of conduct within each agency is the responsibility of the   2.____

   A. agency head
   B. Commissioner of Investigation
   C. Department of Investigation
   D. Inspector General

Questions 3-6.

DIRECTIONS: Questions 3 through 6 are to be answered on the basis of the following information.

Assume that Warehouse X uses the following procedures for receiving stock. When a delivery is received, the stock handler who receives the delivery should immediately unpack and check the delivery. This check is to ensure that the quantity and kinds of stock items delivered match those on the purchase order which had been sent to the vendor. After the delivery is checked, a receiving report is prepared by the same stock handler. This receiving report should include the name of the shipper, the purchase order number, the description of the item, and the actual count or weight of the item. The receiving report, along with the packing slip, should then be checked by the stores clerk against the purchase order to make sure that the quantity received is correct. This is necessary before credit can be obtained from the vendor for any items that are missing or damaged. After the checking is completed, the stock items can be moved to the stockroom.

3. According to the procedures described above, the stock person who receives the delivery should   3._____

    A.   place the unopened delivery in a secure area for checking at a later date
    B.   notify the stores clerk that the delivery has arrived and is ready for checking
    C.   unpack the delivery and check the quantity and types of stock items against the purchase order
    D.   closely examine the outside of the delivery containers for dents and damages

4. According to the procedures described above, credit can be obtained from the vendor   4._____

    A.   *before* the stock handler checks the delivery of stock items
    B.   *after* the stock handler checks the delivery of stock items
    C.   *before* the stores clerk checks the receiving report against the purchase order
    D.   *after* the stores clerk checks the receiving report against the purchase order

5. According to the procedures described above, all of the following information should be included when filling out a receiving report EXCEPT the   5._____

    A.   purchase order number
    B.   name of the shipper
    C.   count or weight of the item
    D.   unit cost per item

6. According to the procedures described above, after the stores clerk has checked the receiving report against the purchase order, the NEXT step is to   6._____

    A.   move the stock items to the stockroom
    B.   return the stock items received to the vendor
    C.   give the stock items to the stock handler for final checking
    D.   file the packing slip for inventory purposes

Questions 7-9.

DIRECTIONS: Questions 7 through 9 are to be answered on the basis of the information given in the following passage.

A filing system for requisition forms used in a warehouse will be of maximum benefit only if it provides ready access to information needed and is not too complex. How effective the system will be depends largely on how well the filing system is organized. A well-organized system usually results in a smooth-running operation.

When setting up a system for filing requisition forms, one effective method would be to first make an alphabetical listing of all the authorized requisitioning agencies. Then file folders should be prepared for each of these agencies and arranged alphabetically in file cabinets. Following this, each agency should be assigned a series of numbers corresponding to those on the blank requisition forms with which they will be supplied. When an agency then submits a requisition and it is filled, the form should be filed in numerical order in the designated agency folder. By using this system, any individual requisition form which is missing from its folder can be easily detected. Regardless of the filing system used, simplicity is essential if the filing system is to be successful.

7. According to the above passage, a filing system is MOST likely to be successful if it is   7.____

   A. alphabetical   B. uncomplicated
   C. numerical   D. reliable

8. According to the above passage, the reason numbers are assigned to each agency is to   8.____

   A. simplify stock issuing procedures
   B. keep a count of all incoming requisition forms
   C. be able to know when a form is missing from its folder
   D. eliminate the need for an alphabetical filing system

9. According to the above passage, which one of the following is an ACCURATE statement   9.____
regarding the establishment of a well-organized filing system?

   A. Requisitioned stock items will be issued at a faster rate.
   B. Stock items will be stored in storage areas alphabetically arranged.
   C. Information concerning ordered stock items will be easily obtainable.
   D. Maximum productivity can be expected from each employee.

Questions 10-13.

DIRECTIONS: Questions 10 through 13 are to be answered SOLELY on the basis of the information in the following paragraph.

On Tuesday, October 21, Protection Agent Williams, on duty at the Jamaica Depot, observed a man jump over the fence and into the parking lot at 2:12 P.M. and run to a car that was parked with the engine running. The man, who limped slightly, opened the car door, jumped into the car, and sped out of the yard. The car was a 1991 gray Buick Electra, license plate 563-JYN, with parking decal No. 6043. The man was white, about 6 feet tall, about 175 pounds, in his mid-20's, with a scar on his left cheek. He wore a blue sportcoat, tan slacks, a white shirt open at the neck with no tie, and brown loafers.

10. What was the color of the car?   10.____

   A. White   B. Blue
   C. Two-tone brown and tan   D. Gray

11. What were the distinguishing personal features of the man who jumped over the fence?   11.____

    A. A scar on the left cheek
    B. Pockmarks on his face
    C. A cast on his left wrist
    D. Bushy eyebrows

12. What was the number on the car's parking decal?   12.____

    A. 1991   B. 673-JYN
    C. 6043   D. 175

13. On what day of the week did the incident occur?   13.____

    A. Monday   B. Tuesday
    C. Wednesday   D. Sunday

14. *It is a violation of rules for a Protection Agent to carry a firearm while on Transit Authority*   14.____
property. The possession of such a weapon, whether carried on the person, in a per-
sonal vehicle, or stored in a locker, can result in charges being filed against the Agent.
According to the above information, the carrying of a firearm

    A. on Authority property by any employee is prohibited
    B. anywhere by an Agent is prohibited under all circumstances
    C. on Authority property by an Agent is prohibited under all circumstances
    D. anywhere by an Authority employee may be reason for charges being filed against that employee

15. *News reporters may enter Authority property if they have the written authorization of a*   15.____
Public Affairs Department official. The Agent on duty must get permission from the Prop-
erty Protection Control Desk before admitting to the property a news person who has no
such written authorization.
If a reporter tells a Protection Agent that she has received permission from the Authority President to enter the property, what is the FIRST thing the Agent should do?

    A. Call the Authority police.
    B. Admit the reporter immediately.
    C. Call the Authority President's office.
    D. Call the Property Protection Control Desk.

Questions 16-20.

DIRECTIONS: Questions 16 through 20 are to be answered SOLELY on the basis of the information in the paragraphs below.

FIRES AND EXTINGUISHERS

There are four classes of fires.

Trash fires, paper fires, cloth fires, wood fires, etc. are classified as Class A fires. Water or
a water-base solution should be used to extinguish Class A fires. They also can be extinguished by covering the combustibles with a multi-purpose dry chemical.

Burning liquids, gasoline, oil, paint, tar, etc. are considered Class B fires. Such fires can be extinguished by smothering or blanketing them. Extinguishers used for Class B fires are Halon, CO_2, or multi-purpose dry chemical. Water tends to spread such fires and should not be used.

Fires in electrical equipment and switchboards are classified as Class C fires. When live electrical equipment is involved, a non-conducting extinguishing agent like CO_2, a multi-purpose dry chemical, or Halon should always be used. Soda-acid or other water-type extinguishers should not be used.

Class D fires consist of burning metals in finely-divided forms like chips, turnings, and shavings. Specially-designed extinguishing agents that provide a smothering blanket or coating should be used to extinguish Class D fires. Multipurpose dry-powder extinguishants are such agents.

16. The ONLY type of extinguishing agent that can be used on any type of fire is   16.____

    A. a multi-purpose, dry-chemical extinguishing agent
    B. soda-acid
    C. water
    D. carbon dioxide

17. A fire in litter swept from a subway car in a yard is MOST likely to be a Class _____ fire.   17.____

    A. A   B. B
    C. C   , D. D

18. Fire coming from the underbody of a subway car is MOST likely to be a Class _____   18.____
fire.

    A. A   B. B
    C. C   D. D

19. Which of the following extinguishing agents should NOT be used in fighting a Class C fire   19.____
involving live electrical equipment?

    A. Halon
    B. Carbon dioxide
    C. A multi-purpose dry chemical
    D. Soda-acid

20. Water is NOT recommended for use on Class B fires because water   20.____

    A. would cool the fire   B. evaporates too quickly
    C. might spread the fire   D. would smother the fire

Questions 21-24.

DIRECTIONS: Questions 21 through 24 are to be answered SOLELY on the basis of the information in the paragraph below.

Protection Agent Brown, working the midnight to 8:00 A.M. tour at the Flushing Bus Depot, discovered a fire at 2:17 A.M. in Bus No. 4651, which was parked in the southeast portion of the depot yard. He turned in an alarm to the Fire Department from Box 3297 on the nearby street at 2:18 A.M. At 2:20 A.M., he called the Property Protection Control Desk and reported the fire and his action to Line Supervisor Wilson. Line Supervisor Wilson instructed Agent Brown to lock his booth and go to the fire alarm box to direct the fire companies. The first arriving companies were Engine 307 and Ladder 154. Brown directed them to the burning bus. Two minutes later, at 2:23 A.M. Battalion Chief Welsh arrived from Battalion 14. The fire had made little headway. It was extinguished in about two minutes. Brown then wrote a fire report for submittal to Line Supervisor Wilson.

21. What was the FIRST thing Protection Agent Brown did after observing the fire? He

    A. called Battalion Chief Welsh
    B. called the Fire Dispatcher
    C. transmitted an alarm from a nearby alarm box
    D. called 911

21.____

22. In what part of the yard was the burning bus?

    A. Northeast section   B. Southwest end
    C. Northwest part   D. Southeast portion

22.____

23. What time did Agent Brown call Line Supervisor Wilson?

    A. 2:18 PM   B. 2:20 AM
    C. 2:29 AM   D. 2:36 AM

23.____

24. Which of the following CORRECTLY describes the sequence of Agent Brown's actions? He

    A. saw the fire, turned in an alarm, called the Property Protection Control Desk, directed the fire companies to the fire, and wrote a report
    B. called the Property Protection Control Desk, directed the fire apparatus, directed Chief Welsh, and wrote a report
    C. called Line Supervisor Wilson, turned in an alarm, waited by the burning bus, and directed the fire companies
    D. called Line Supervisor Wilson, directed the firefighters, waited for instructions from Line Supervisor Wilson, and wrote a report

24.____

Questions 25-26.

DIRECTIONS: Questions 25 and 26 are to be answered SOLELY on the basis of the following paragraph and rule.

Protection Agents may admit to Transit Authority headquarters only persons with Transit Authority passes, persons with job appointment letters, and persons who have permission to enter from Transit Authority officials.

During his tour in the Authority's headquarters lobby, Protection Agent Williams admitted to the building 326 persons with Authority passes and 41 persons with job appointment letters. He telephoned authorized officials for permission to admit 14 others, 13 of whom were granted permission and entered and one of whom was denied permission. He also turned away two persons who wanted to enter to sell to employees merchandise for their personal use, and one person who appeared inebriated.

25. How many persons did Agent Williams admit to the building?   25.____

    A. 326   B. 367
    C. 380   D. 382

26. To how many persons did Agent Williams refuse admittance?   26.____

    A. 4   B. 13
    C. 14   D. 41

Questions 27-30.

DIRECTIONS: Questions 27 through 30 are to be answered on the basis of the information contained in the following instructions on LOST PROPERTY.

LOST PROPERTY

All inquiries for information regarding lost property will be referred to the Lost Property Office. Any Station Department employee finding a lost article, of any description, will immediately hand it over to the railroad clerk in the nearest 24-hour booth of the station where the article is found. The clerk must give the employee a receipt for the article. Should a passenger hand over a lost article to a cleaner, the cleaner will offer to escort the passenger to the nearest 24-hour booth in order that a receipt may be given by the railroad clerk there. If the passenger declines, the cleaner will accept the lost article without giving a receipt and proceed as described above. Each employee who receives lost property will be held responsible for it unless he produces a receipt for it from another employee. Should any lost property disappear, the last employee who signed for it will be held strictly accountable.

27. If a cleaner turns in a lost article to a railroad clerk in the nearest 24-hour booth, he should make sure that he   27.____

    A. gets a receipt for the article
    B. notifies his supervisor about the lost article
    C. finds out the name of the owner of the article
    D. writes a report on the incident

28. If a lost article disappears after a cleaner has properly turned it in to the railroad clerk in the nearest 24-hour booth, the one who will be held accountable is the   28.____

    A. person who found the lost article
    B. cleaner who turned in the article
    C. supervisor in charge of the station
    D. last employee to sign a receipt for the article

29. A passenger finds a lost article and gives it to a cleaner. The cleaner gives the passenger a receipt. The cleaner's action was

    A. *proper* because the passenger was relieved of any responsibility for the lost article
    B. *improper* because the cleaner should have offered to escort the passenger to the nearest 24-hour booth
    C. *proper* because the cleaner is required to give the passenger a receipt
    D. *improper* because the cleaner should have sent the passenger to the Lost Property Office

29.____

30. A cleaner finds a five dollar bill on a crowded station platform. Three passengers who see him pick it up rush up and claim the money. The first passenger said he had just taken a roll of bills out of his pocket and must have dropped it. The second said he had just given two five dollar bills to his wife, and she had dropped one of them. The third said he had a hole in his pocket and the bill fell out of it. The cleaner should

    A. give the five dollar bill to the second passenger because he had his wife as a witness
    B. give the five dollar bill to the third passenger because he had a hole in his pocket
    C. keep the five dollar bill
    D. bring the five dollar bill to the railroad clerk in the nearest 24-hour booth

30.____

KEY (CORRECT ANSWERS)

1.	A		16.	A
2.	D		17.	A
3.	C		18.	C
4.	D		19.	D
5.	D		20.	C
6.	A		21.	C
7.	B		22.	D
8.	C		23.	B
9.	C		24.	A
10.	D		25.	C
11.	A		26.	A
12.	C		27.	A
13.	B		28.	D
14.	C		29.	B
15.	D		30.	D
